How the
Stock
Markets
Work

How the Stock Markets Work

A GUIDE TO THE INTERNATIONAL MARKETS

COLIN CHAPMAN

RANDOM HOUSE

BUSINESS BOOKS

First published in 1994 by Century Limited
This edition first published in 1999 by
Random House Business Books

Random House Business Books
The Random House Group,
20 Vauxhall Bridge Road, London SW1V 2SA

Random House Australia (Pty) Limited
20 Alfred Street, Milsons Point, Sydney
New South Wales 2061, Australia

Random House New Zealand Limited
18 Poland Road, Glenfield
Auckland 10, New Zealand

Random House (Pty) Limited
Endulini, 5A Jubilee Road, Parktown 2193, South Africa

Random House UK Limited Reg. No. 954009

Papers used by Random House are natural, recyclable products
made from wood grown in sustainable forests. The
manufacturing processes conform to the environmental
regulations of the country of origin.

ISBN 0 7126 8472 7

Typeset by SX Composing DTP, Rayleigh, Essex
Printed in Great Britain by
Biddles Ltd, Guildford and King's Lynn

Companies, institutions and other organizations wishing to make bulk purchases
of books published by Random House should contact their local bookstore or
Random House direct:
Special Sales Director
Random House, 20 Vauxhall Bridge Road, London SW1V 2SA
Tel 0171 840 8470   Fax 0171 828 6681
www.randomhouse.co.uk
businessbooks@randomhouse.co.uk

To Simon, Laura, Ben and Max

Contents

Introduction and Acknowledgements

When the first edition of this book was published 13 years ago, the Internet was almost unknown, and the idea that it might become a household word by the turn of the century was unthinkable.

The stock markets, and particularly the Stock Exchange in London, were accessible only to a minority who could afford them. They were housed in grand stone edifices, constructed to symbolize solidity and strength, the twin pillars of the Establishment, of which they were part. Share trading, more often raucous than docile, took place inside their portals, by law. In most markets, trading outside the exchange was forbidden. It was a people business, and survived and grew on the basis of human relationships and trust.

As we entered the new millenium the London Stock Exchange was undergoing further momentous change. Its members decided to end all those years of history as an independent body owned by its members, and to become a limited company like many of those whose shares trade under its banner. This led the British government to end the Exchange's historical role as a regulator, and to transfer these powers to the Financial Services Authority.

With few exceptions, the only people left in the exchange buildings are administrators and regulators. Share trading takes place electronically wherever there is a telephone line. Each financial centre has a number of privately owned dealing rooms, some the size of a football field, but it is equally possible to buy and sell shares from a cottage in a remote hamlet or from a mobile telephone on board a yacht in the Ionian Sea. Every buyer and every seller, every trader and every market maker is linked digitally by telephone, data lines or the Internet.

Record numbers of people are trading shares directly, many as part of a long-term savings strategy, some as an intellectual challenge to beat the market and to make money, a few as a gamble more likely to pay off in the long run than backing a horse on the race track. Over the period during which this book has been in print, through seven editions, equity investment has proved the best form of saving, out-stripping bonds, property, government savings schemes, building society or bank deposits, and pleasure-related investments such as stamps, antiques and old cars.

In addition to those who trade directly, almost everyone has part of their future tied up in the stock markets. The better off will have money in mutual funds or unit trusts, and other collective investments. A greater percentage of the world's people will have money in life assurance and pension schemes. Whether private or government-controlled, the bil-lions of whatever currency tied up in these schemes will be placed on the international financial markets, for such is the interdependency of nations since the collapse of communism and the growth of globalization. Even the world's destitute will have some dependency on the capital markets, because international organizations like the World Bank, the International Development Finance Corporation, and the European Bank for Reconstruction and Development raise their funds through the global network of financial inter-change.

Yet if all our futures are tied in some way to the world's financial markets and their well-being, and if the sensational growth of the Internet makes buying and selling shares, bonds and other financial instruments easier and cheaper, that does not mean there is anything approaching equality of access. Whereas access was restricted two decades ago to those with money and connections, the limits now are more likely to be imposed by age, attitude, education and environ-ment. Lack of education about the financial markets, in my view, is the greatest handicap. Education in economics and finance tends to be restricted to those specializing in these areas at tertiary level. The result is that the majority of the people in most countries are taught little or nothing about how money works. Doctors, dentists, teachers and media folk are just as likely to fall into this category as those leav-ing school at sixteen.

Unfortunately the world's stock exchanges have contributed little towards improving this state of affairs, and governments, national and local, have not helped either. Scouring the list of courses available at public educational institutions to the residents of the City of London, I found not one devoted to the workings of the London Stock Exchange. Inevitably there were many opportunities to study aromatherapy, reflexology, and folklore and mythology. It may be that if only a quarter of the hundreds of millions of pounds spent on financial regulation in Britain – much of it squandered on inefficient and incompetent bureaucracies – had been used for family financial education, then the pensions and mortgage mis-selling debacles which the regulators were unable to prevent might not have occurred.

This seventh edition of *How the Stock Markets Work* has been restructured and rewritten to reflect the new age, and to take into account the impact of globalization and the Internet. The Internet has made some aspects of research much easier, but it has still been necessary to visit the major financial centres, and to talk with investment professionals. My thanks to them, and to librarians in London and New York who have facilitated access to essential documentation. And, of course, to Susan Grice, whose ability to spot split infinitives and worthless clichés is as strong as ever.

1 Owning Shares

*'Price is not the transforming event. The
transforming event is the ability to deliver
personalized information to the customer in real time,
at virtually no cost'* – David Pottrick, chief executive
of Charles Schwab

Everyone should own shares or bonds. It is the best form of
long-term saving. It is the only way of making reasonably
sure that the money you have today will have value when you
and your dependents are older. This is not to say that your
savings and investments should all be on the stock markets.
It probably makes sense to own your own home, if you can
afford the mortgage and if you are not planning to move frequently. And it is sensible to keep some cash handy on
deposit earning interest should you need it.

But beyond high-interest deposit accounts and home ownership, the stock markets provide the most flexible and
rewarding means of investment. This is not a statement that
I or anyone else would have made 20, even 10 years ago, but
so much has changed on the stock markets in the last few
years of the nineties.

Shares may now be bought or sold more cheaply than most
other investments, and in particular insurance policies, unit
trusts, mutual funds, property bonds, or any of the wretched
endowment policies and collective investments that avaricious and determined salesmen continue to try and force us
to sign up to. Thanks to globalization and electronic dealing
systems shares may also be bought and sold more quickly
than other forms of investment. It may take weeks to sell a
property or to retire a savings plan without a penalty, and
days to cash in a poorly performing insurance policy or unit
trust, but unwanted shares can be sold in seconds. There is
always a buyer and a price. Similarly it may cost a large sum

of money in commission and management charges to hold unit trusts and insurance-related investments; whereas share ownership requires you pay a small commission only when you buy and sell.

Moreover if you buy the wrong shares, or sell your shares at the wrong time it can only be through your own misjudgement. As with most things in life, it is possible to get advice to avoid making silly mistakes. This is not true of collective investments, where you are dependent on others for the safety and performance of the funds in which you have invested. Since fund managers are highly paid and enjoy comfortable lifestyles, it may seem reasonable to suppose that money managed by them will yield a better return than money managed by you. Unfortunately, in recent years, this has not proved the case, with the result that tens of thousands of people have decided to switch to do-it-yourself investment, and buy and sell shares directly themselves.

Nowhere is this trend more prevalent than in the United States, where in 1999 the amount being saved in mutual funds was down 40 per cent from the previous year. The principal reason for public disillusionment with funds is their high charges and poor performance. In America during 1998 the average equity fund rose 14 per cent – about half of the rate of return on the shares that make up the Standard and Poor Index. In Europe the return was even worse. 1998 was not an exceptionally bad year, just the continuation of a trend.

A detailed study conducted by Barclays Capital, a subsidiary of the British high-street bank, found that provided shares are held for a period of three years historically they have produced better returns than high-interest deposit accounts or bonds. The study took a long view, studying 80 years of performance since the end of the First World War in 1918, and looking at both short and long periods within this epoch. Where investments were held for a decade or more, shares outperformed deposits in 97 per cent of ten-year spells, and did better than bonds for 94 per cent of the time. Even for short periods of only two years the incidence of shares performing better than either bonds or deposits was 70 per cent. One notable exception was after the 1987 global stock market crash, when it took six years for an investment in shares to outperform a high-interest deposit.

Another study by the securities house, Credit Suisse First Boston, found that during a 12-month period in 1998–9 government bonds in Britain were a better investment than equity shares, generating total returns of 22 per cent, compared with 11 per cent. But over the long haul the picture again is totally different. A £100 investment made in gilt-edged securities in 1918 at the end of the First World War would have grown to just £13,000 by the end of 1998. Had it been invested in popular shares in the major companies the £100 would have grown to more than £1 million. Neither figure takes any account of annual inflation, but it is clear that those who bought equities would have been the only real winners.

So why did interest in shares not develop sooner? Shares used to be the preserve of the rich. Buying and selling them was expensive, and had to be carried out through a closed shop of stockbrokers who preferred to deal with account holders of the same social class as themselves. Those who fared best on the stock markets were those in the know, or who had inside information. There was a clear pecking order for access to information. At the top of the list was the stockbroker himself and his most favoured clients, people who either did him favours or who traded often, thus providing him with high commissions. Next came people with connections, travelling companions in the first-class compartments of commuter trains to the 'stockbroker belt', and financial editors of major newspapers who could be depended upon to write favourably about the shares his number one group had just bought, thereby pushing the price up. Before the newspaper went to press, the financial editor would, of course, help himself to a few shares. The third layer for access to information were the readers of the broadsheet newspapers, particularly the *Financial Times*, *The Times* and the *Wall Street Journal*, and at the bottom of the pile came everyone else. With this as the scenario, it is hardly surprising that Joe Public felt excluded from the stock markets. The average family was no more likely to buy shares than to venture on to the Yorkshire grouse moors on 12 August, the start of the British shooting season, or to enter the Royal Enclosure at Ascot, Britain's most exclusive racecourse.

In fact a survey carried out by MORI for the London Stock

Exchange found that, despite the evidence to the contrary and benefiting from years of privatization's and demutualizations, most people still consider shares to be an unwise long-term investment. The MORI survey, released to coincide with the launch of a Share Aware Campaign in 1999, found that 64 per cent of people have yet to be convinced that shares provide a better form of long-term investment than savings accounts.

According to figures collected by *Proshare*, which promotes equity investment, share ownership levels in Britain still lag behind the US. Only 27 per cent of the UK population own shares, whereas in the US the figure stands at around 40 per cent. The public still views the stock market as risky, despite the claim from *Proshare* that between 1988 and 1997 equity markets had an average annual return of 15.7 per cent.

I agree with Justin Urquhart Stewart, of Barclays Stockbrokers, who argues that the process of dealing in shares needs to be demystified.

> It's depressing that people still think deposit accounts make better investments. The US is much more clued-up about share dealing than the UK, but it is hardly surprising given the poor level of financial education available in Britain. We learn about home economics, but practical financial education is not even on the school syllabus.

The survey led to a *Proshare* campaign presented by Charlie Dimmock, the television gardener. The stock exchange, keen to show it is not an all-male preserve, said Ms Dimmock was chosen because she was a woman and because of the analogy between growing plants and investing for the long term.

It is an irony that in the forties and the fifties, while the punters were excluded from the stock markets, they were indirectly contributing to the growing wealth of the privileged few. Each week the 'man from the Pru', a sallow foot soldier from what was then Britain's largest life assurance company, would call on homes in the mean streets of the country's towns and villages and collect a few pence towards a savings scheme. After the salesman's commission and other costs, the residue would be invested on the stock markets. The Prudential, and others who practised street investment such as the Liverpool Victoria, Pearl Assurance and the United Friendly, were prime and favoured clients for the coterie of stockbrokers in the City of London – each treated each other well.

Thus collective investments were born on the argument that small people – later more politely referred to as small investors – could more safely access the stock markets through giant institutions. The collective might of these organizations could wield the kind of power in trading that no individual could aspire to. Rather than risk investing in any one share, those holding collective investments could have their savings managed by experts who would achieve better results.

The theory made sound economic sense, and for a while it worked. But as the financial services industry grew larger, and greedier, it began to sow the seeds for its own self-destruction. Many, if not most, financial products designed for the mass markets were sold by commission agents, who preferred to use the euphemism of financial adviser. Most of them were rewarded not from fees geared to the quality of their advice, but from a sizeable cut of the first 18 months' contribution. Many so-called financial advisers sold families packages that were totally inappropriate, a practice that later became known as mis-selling, and was to cost the companies dearly.

In parallel with this the British government, in common with many others, burdened the financial services industry with a complex set of regulations, which added greatly to costs. Some of the new rules were sensible and long overdue, such as a total ban on insider trading, which was made a criminal offence. Others were poorly drafted, hard to enforce, and an encouragement to unnecessary bureaucracy.

It became hard to run collective investment schemes profitably, but the burden of regulation was not the only cost pressure. The greater force pushing prices skywards was that created by inflated salaries paid in financial centres like the City of London. It became commonplace for City fund managers and other executives to earn in excess of £200,000 a year, supplemented by an annual bonus of an equivalent amount. In Wall Street pay is much higher, sometimes four times higher. The only way to avoid losses has been to increase charges to the investor.

This development coincided with a revolution in technology. It became possible for the private individual to buy and sell shares, if not on equal terms with the professional traders, at least swiftly and efficiently, and at reasonable cost. At the same time it also became easy for the individual investor to obtain a great deal of relevant information free of charge.

The technologies that were the catalyst for change were not particularly new: the first was the telephone, and the second was the internet. What was new was the way in which one company, Charles Schwab, utilized these technologies for share trading by individuals, and then took the market by storm, transforming the industry as it did so.

Charles Schwab started his share trading business to serve cities and towns across America through bustling Main Street branch offices known as share shops. There, over a cup of coffee, a browse through the *Wall Street Journal*, and a look at the New York Stock Exchange prices running across a ticker, investors could buy and sell shares. Some sought advice from the Schwab staff on hand; others acted on their own.

By the early 1990s the firm had become the largest out-of-town broker in the United States, but was hardly a threat to the titans of Wall Street, such as the giant Merrill Lynch Pierce Venner and Smith, known throughout the financial world as 'the thundering herd'.

Then Charles Schwab began to develop its telephone business, building call centres to accept buy or sell orders from customers, and executing trades immediately through its own team of traders based at the New York Stock Exchange. It also acquired the British company, Sharelink, founded in Birmingham by the entrepeneur David Jones, to cash in on the interest in share trading created by the wave of privatizations in the years of Margaret Thatcher's Conservative government. Until Sharelink arrived it had not been easy for ordinary Britons to trade shares, for the reasons mentioned earlier. Jones, helped by technologists from the University of Cambridge, created what, in effect, was a share trading factory on the first floor of an unpretentious building in a dreary quarter of the city mostly inhabited by insurance companies. Few people gave him much of a chance, and the London Stock Exchange, retreating only slowly from its old traditions of privilege and pretence, did its best to crush the business through a variety of legal manouevres. But Jones won through, built the business, and sold out to Schwab.

Charles Schwab's real breakthrough came with web trading, when its technology group came up with new software that allowed a server to take an order from a Web browser on a personal computer, route it through the company's sophisticated back-end systems and mainframes, execute it, and send a confirmation back to the buyer's PC. It now processes more trades online than through traditional means. The numbers of people using the Schwab web site are little short of astonishing. At the end of 1999 it was recording 76 million visitors each day, and had grabbed 42 per cent of the online business, adding 1.3 million new email account customers in the year.

Schwab has not been without competition, but it has come from new companies rather than the financial services industry establishment. One of its major competitors is E-Trade, which has its beginnings at the Cambridge Science Park, and now operates in the United States, Britain, Australia and New Zealand.

Trading shares could now not be easier. Using one of the two major web browsers, Microsoft Explorer or Netscape Navigator, you open the Charles Schwab or E-Trade web site, select the market in which you wish to trade – for example United Kingdom – and then log on using your account number and password. This will take you directly to the page containing the details of your account, including the latest prices of any shares you already own, and their value. If you wish to trade you enter the name of the company whose shares you wish to buy or sell, and the number of shares to be traded. The next page to appear will provide you with the cost of the transaction, and ask you if you wish to confirm. If you accept the deal, the trade will be carried out and confirmed back to you.

It is as easy, or easier, than purchasing an airline ticket, and a lot easier than buying a train ride. If you do not have computer access, buying and selling by phone is still available. All you need to know is what shares are, what makes them valuable one day and less valuable the next, how to pick and choose them, and when to buy and sell. But first a little history.

2   History

'*The howling of the wolf, the grunting of the hog,
the braying of the ass, the nocturnal wooing of the cat,
all these in unison could not be more hideous than the
noise which these beings make in the Stock*' –
Anonymous commentator on the scene in Change
Alley, London in 1695.

'*Stock-jobbing is knavish in its private practice, and
treason in its public*' – Daniel Defoe.

'*Dictum meum pactum – My word is my bond*' –
Handbook of the London Stock Exchange.

For most the stock markets epitomize the concept of risk and
reward. With not too much of the former, and the chance of
achieving a fair amount of the latter, the investor can be on
the road to riches. This has been true throughout the three
centuries of stock market activity.

Those who took a billion-pound risk in investing in satellite television in Britain at the end of the twentieth century
were opting for the same choice as the few backers prepared
to chance £3,200 apiece on the *Concepcion* adventure in
1686. Then, a whiskery sea captain from Boston called Phips
sought investors for an expedition to the north coast of
Hispaniola to salvage a sunken galleon. Nine months later the
backers reaped their reward – £250,000 worth of fine silver.

Then as now another major threat to any investment has
been that people cheat. There are big cheats and little cheats,
and only a few of them have passed through the dock of the
Old Bailey. The excitement that greeted the trial in London
of the Guinness Five in 1990 or the humiliation of the president of the House of Nomura a year later – or the imprisonment of Ivan Boesky and Michael Milken in New York,
Ronald Li in Hong Kong, and Nick Leeson in Singapore –

was only a latter-day repeat of events in Britain in the late seventeenth century.

The collapse of Barings in 1995, a famous London investment bank, set regulators searching for new solutions and tougher rules. It was much the same in 1697, when, following a wave of market-rigging and insider trading, the British government brought in an Act designed to 'restrain the number and ill-practice of brokers and stockjobbers'.

This followed a report from a Parliamentary Commission set up a year earlier which had discovered that:

> the pernicious art of stockjobbing hath, of late, so perverted the end design of Companies and Corporations, erected for the introducing or carrying on of manufactures, to the private profit of the first projectors, that the privileges granted to them have commonly been made no other use of – but to sell again, with advantage, to innocent men.

As a result of the 1697 Act all stockbrokers and stockjobbers had to be licensed before they plied their trade in the coffee shops, walks and alleys near the Royal Exchange in London. These licences were limited to 100 and were granted by the Lord Mayor of London and the Court of Aldermen. They cost only £2, and entitled the licensee to wear a specially struck silver medal embossed with the Royal Arms, once he had taken an oath that he would 'truly and faithfully execute and perform the office and employment of a broker between party and party, without fraud or collusion'.

The rules of operation were strict. Brokers were not allowed to deal on their own behalf, but only for clients. They could not hold any options for more than three days without facing the certainty of permanent expulsion. Commission was limited to 5 per cent, or less. Anyone who tried to operate as a broker without a licence was, if caught, exposed to three days in the City pillory.

Muscovy and Company

The trade in shares began with City traders and merchants spreading the risk of two major entrepreneurial journeys: an attempt to investigate the prospects offered by the uncharted White Sea and Arctic Circle, and a voyage to India and the East Indies via the Cape of Good Hope.

These ventures were to lead to the world's first two public companies: the Muscovy Company and the East India Company. Until then companies had been privately owned businesses, or partnerships between individuals. These companies were new and different. Their owners contributed money to what was called 'joint stock', and these contributions were verified through certificates which became known as shares. If later unwanted these shares were freely transferable to anyone who would pay them at a price acceptable to both buyer and seller.

The Muscovy Company was a brave, risky and costly venture by Sebastian Cabot in 1553 to attempt to find a north-east trade route from Britain to China and what was then known as the Orient. Cabot and his crew would take the physical risk, but others were needed to share the financial risk. As one of the first shareholders explained at the time:

> Every man willing to bee of the societie, should disburse the portion of twentie and five pounds a piece: so that in a short time, by this means, the sum of six thousand pounds being gathered, three ships were brought.

Two of the three ships that formed the expedition sank off Norway, and things looked bleak for the 250 merchants putting up £25 each. But one of the project leaders did make it to Moscow, where he persuaded Ivan the Terrible to sign a trade agreement. This did yield some returns, though not what might have been achieved had they been able to get through the Arctic icecap to Asia.

The East India Company was more successful, and was the first company to find shareholders prepared to put up money on a substantial scale. It needed modern, armed ships for the difficult and dangerous voyage to the Orient, and a home base of substantial docks in London. Although some ships sank on voyages, and the company hovered close to bankruptcy in its early days, it managed to raise over £1.6 million over 17 years. As the silk and spice trade developed, those who had invested in the original stock enjoyed returns of 40 per cent a year.

This led enterprising developers to realize quickly that raising capital through shares was a good way to fund less risky ventures which were still hard for one person, however rich, to finance. Why not create more joint-stock companies for domestic projects? One of the earliest was established by Francis, Earl of Bedford, to fulfil his bold plan to drain the Fens. The aim of this ambitious scheme was to create thousands of hectares of additional fertile agricultural land, and to provide London with its first supply of fresh water. So others were persuaded to add to his own £100,000 contribution, and in 1609 The 'Government and Company of the New River brought from Chadwell and Amwell to London' was founded. It become Britain's first water stock. Although the water company operations were bought out by the Metropolitan Water Board in 1904, the company still exists as the oldest to be quoted on the London Stock Exchange.

The Stock Exchange Official List

By the end of the seventeenth century there were a number of large joint stock companies, and substantial dealing in their shares. The historian W. R. Scott estimated that by 1695 there were 140 joint stock companies, with a total market capitalization of £4.5 million. When people wanted to buy and sell shares in these companies, the place to do it was usually one of two coffee houses in the heart of the City of London. One was called Garraway's and the other Jonathan's, and both were near Change Alley, a haunt favoured by City merchants and traders. Change Alley is still to be found today in the narrow spit of land between Cornhill and Threadneedle Street, close to the Bank of England.

The patrons of the coffee establishments of the seventeenth century had style and colour. There were no grey suits to be seen; even the tinkers dressed up. The atmosphere was convivial, the talk was of adventure and new ideas. The British empire was expanding, and there was money to be made, and shares to be bought and sold. Over coffee you could also run your eye down a sheet of paper containing the latest prices of most commodities, and of those shares traded. The name of this daily sheet was also an accurate description of it: 'The Course of the Exchange and Other Things'. It was to be the precursor of greater publications to come – the *Stock Exchange Daily Official List*, the *Financial Times* and the *Wall Street Journal*. A writer of the day set the scene:

> The centre of the jobbing is in the Kingdom of Exchange Alley and its adjacencies: the limits are easily surrounded in about a Minute and a half stepping out of Jonathan's into the Alley, you turn your face full South, moving on a few paces, and then turn-ing Due East, you advance to Garraway's; from there going out at the other Door, you go on still East into Birchin Lane and then halting a little at the Sword-Blade Bank to do much mischief in fervent Words, you immediately face to the North, enter Cornhill, visit two or three petty Provinces there in your way West; and thus having Boxed your Compass, and sail'd round the whole Stock Jobbing Globe, you turn into Jonathan's again; and so, as most of the great Follies of Life oblige us to do, you end just where you began.

South Sea Bubble

This coffee society was to thrive for more than 50 years, and by 1720 Change Alley and its coffee houses were thronged with brokers. It was the place to be. Throughout the day the narrow streets were impassable, because of the throng of lords and ladies in their carriages. The Act regulating and restricting their access to the narrow streets lapsed by default, because nobody took any notice of it, and no one tried to enforce it. The scene is described in an eighteenth-century ballad:

> Then stars and garters did appear
> Among the meaner rabble
> To buy and sell, to see and hear
> The Jews and Gentiles squabble,
> The greatest ladies thither came
> And plied in chariots daily,
> Or pawned their jewels for a sum
> To venture in the Alley.

The principal attraction was the excitement caused by the booming share price of the South Sea Company, which started to be sold in 1720 at £128 each, and swiftly rose as euphoria about the company's prospects was spread both by brokers and by the government. By March the price had risen to £330, by May it was £550, and by 24 June it had reached an insane £1,050. The South Sea Company had been set up nine years earlier by the British government, ostensibly with the aim of opening up trade and markets for new commodities in South America. It also had another purpose, which, these days, has a familiar ring about it. By converting it to a public company, rather than a government department, it reduced the Treasury's public debt by £9 million.

For eight years the company was moribund and unprofitable. Its shares were dormant. It had only one contract of any size: to supply black slaves to Latin America. The government then adopted the concept of privatization of a state-owned concern, something much more audacious than the sales of British Telecom or British Gas over 250 years later. It offered shares in the South Sea Company to the public, hoping that it would raise enough money to wipe out the entire National Debt of some £31 million.

The government was persuaded to do this by a wily operator, Sir John Blunt, who was a director of the company and effectively underwrote the issue. An underwriter in the financial markets guarantees that if there are not enough people willing to buy the shares on offer, he will do so at a discount. The issue was made on a 'partly paid' basis; which means an investor has only to find a small proportion at the time, but then pays for the full cost in instalments. The offer was heavily oversubscribed, and many people who had hoped to get South Sea shares missed out. There was considerable irritation when it was discovered that Blunt's acquaintances, and other people of influence, had been allotted an extra allocation, a circumstance that was to repeat itself in Britain during the Thatcher privatizations.

The government realized it would be possible to raise even more money on the strength of the supposed bright future of the South Sea Company. To encourage wider share ownership, the company was encouraged to make loans to the public to buy its shares, with the loans secured on the shares themselves. Three centuries later the practice emerged again with the issue of junk bonds, discussed in a later chapter.

Sir John Blunt proved adept at adopting the techniques of public relations to push the share price up. There were hints of lavish dividends to come, prominent people offered thinly disguised bribes to buy shares and talk about it. Even the peace negotiations under way with Spain were frequently deployed for propaganda purposes, since the prospect of an end to conflict meant more trade with South America.

The astute reader will by now have guessed the inevitable outcome. The smart money, including that invested by the prime minister, Sir Robert Walpole, sold out at the peak of the boom. The Prince of Wales, the Duke of Argyll, the chancellor of the Exchequer and many Members of Parliament made handsome profits. The bubble burst, and triggered off the first ever bear market. Within eight weeks of rising above the £1,000 mark, the share price plunged to £175. By December it had sunk to £124, bringing ruin to those who had seen the South Sea Company as the chance of a lifetime. There was an outcry, forcing the government to introduce legislation in the shape of the Bubble Act, designed to prevent a rash of similar speculative ventures from springing up. There was the inevitable Parliamentary inquiry, which concluded that the accounts had been falsified and a government minister bribed. One of the few public figures to pay a penalty was the hapless chancellor of the exchequer. Before he had a chance to enjoy his £800,000 capital gain, he was committed to the Tower upon being found guilty of the 'most notorious, dangerous and infamous corruption'.

It was – and remains – the most fabled episode in British financial history. It took a while for investors to recover their nerves, and it was a long time before the fledgling stock market got back into its stride. Indeed it was the next century before another large crop of joint-stock companies was formed, and this only came about because of an acute shortage of capital for major projects both at home and abroad.

Mines, Railways, Canals

By 1824, the end of the cyclical trade depression, there were

156 companies quoted on the London Stock Exchange, with a market capitalization of £47.9 million. In the following twelve months interest in investment increased sharply. Prospectuses were issued for no less than 624 companies with capital requirements of £372 million. The largest group were general investment companies, mostly with extensive interests overseas, which raised £52 million. Canals and railways came next, raising £44 million, followed by mining companies with £38 million and insurance, a new industry, with £35 million.

The railways proved to be a great benefit for the promotion of investment, even if most of the investors lost their money. The Duke of Wellington had opposed the development of railways, arguing imperiously that 'railroads will only encourage the lower classes to move about needlessly'. His words proved to be prescient. Not only did people start to travel, but the upper classes living outside London were spurred into owning shares. A new word entered the financial vocabulary: stag, a person who applies for an allotment of shares with the clear intention of selling them to someone else before having to meet the cost of buying them.

The stags were out in force in 1836 when George Hudson, a bluff Yorkshireman, raised £300,000 for the York and North Midland Railway under the slogan 'Mak' all t'railways coom t'York'. The £50 shares were oversubscribed and quickly traded at a premium of £4 each. Within three years the line was opened, and the bells of York Minster pealed out in joyful celebration. Much of the joy was shortlived. So many railway lines spread out across the country that many rail companies could not pay the wages of the train drivers, even less dividends for shareholders. Many companies were overcapitalized, but instead of returning the cash to shareholders, managements found other ways to use the surplus funds, much to the chagrin of investors.

Despite these setbacks, by 1842 there were 66 railway companies quoted on the London Stock Exchange, with a capital of almost £50 million. During the boom in railway issues, the *Economist* was moved to write an editorial, which, with a change of name and date, might well have fitted into the British Telecom era of 1985: 'Everybody is in the stocks now (sic),' it purred. 'Needy clerks, poor tradesmen's apprentices, discarding serving men and bankrupts – all have entered the ranks of the great moneyed interest.'

Provincial stock markets were also established. Local investment opportunities were featured in the advertisements for share auctions which regularly appeared in a Liverpool newspaper after about 1827. It was quite usual to use a property auction as the opportunity to dispose of a parcel of shares. By the middle of 1845, regional stock exchanges had been formed in 12 towns and cities, from Bristol in the south, to Newcastle in the north, with Yorkshire claiming the greatest number. But only five of them were to survive the trading slump of 1845 to become permanent institutions.

Government Debt

All through this period government debt had been growing. Compensation to slave-owners, whose slaves had been freed, the cost of the Crimean War and the purchase by the government of the national telegraph system, combined to blow out the deficit.

Raising the cash to fund it provided the most lucrative and reliable form of income for stockbrokers. By 1860, British funds amounted to more than all the other quoted securities combined, and created by far the widest market in the Exchange. Government stocks, or bonds, were bought daily from the Treasury by the City figure called the Government Broker, who then sold them on in the market-place. The idea was that these stocks, to become known much later as gilt-edged securities, would be used to reduce or even eradicate the National Debt. Of course issuing these bonds had the opposite effect, because they added to the debt, but they quickly became a way of funding unpopular measures. Had the government not been able to borrow money through these tradable bonds, it would have had to resort to taxation.

It was not long before local authorities also jumped on the bandwagon. The City of Dublin was the first to raise money through bonds, followed by Edinburgh, Glasgow and the Metropolitan Board of Works.

The First Exchange

By this time the brokers and other money dealers had long since left their colourful but damp pitches in Change Alley. The friendly coffee houses had become too crowded for comfort, and everyone knew everyone else's business. The nature of the customers also changed, as Change Alley played host to people described by the established professionals as 'riff-raff'. When Jonathan's was finally burnt down after a series of major fires around 1748, the broking industry sought refuge in New Jonathan's, rebuilt in Threadneedle Street, where they were charged a sixpence a day entrance fee, a sum sufficient to discourage tinkers, money-lenders and the other parasites who had frequented the previous premises. Soon afterwards they put a sign over the door: The Stock Exchange.

The stock market continued to operate in this way, more or less as a club, for 30 years, until its members decided something more formal was needed. On 7 February 1801 its days as the Stock Exchange ended and it was shut down, to reopen one month later as the 'Stock Subscription Room'. The *per diem* entry fee was stopped, but to join members had to be elected, and then to pay a fee of ten guineas, and risk a fine of two guineas if they were found guilty of 'disorderly conduct', the penalty going to charity. There does not seem to be an accurate record of how many charities benefited from this provision, or how many fines were levied.

The Stock Subscription Room had a short life, for members quickly decided it was too small, and in the same year laid the foundation stone for a new building in Capel Court. This stone records that this was also the 'first year of the union between Great Britain and Ireland', and notes that the building was being 'erected by private subscription for transaction of the business in the public funds'.

Not all members of the public were impressed by this new monument; the old lady who sold cups of tea and sweet buns outside Capel Court moved away because, she said: 'the Stock Exchange is such a wicked place'. But with monuments come tablets, and it was not long before members were forced to draw up new rules of operation. Adopted in 1812, these still form the basis of the present-day rule book. Neither members nor their wives could be engaged in any other business, failures had to be chalked up above the clock immediately so that there could be a fair distribution of assets to creditors, and members were informed that they had to give up 'rude and trifling practices which have long disgraced the Stock Exchange'.

The Capel Court building was to last a century and a half, and in the end it was not size but ancient communications that made it unworkable. The decision was taken to rebuild, and a new 'state-of-the-art' 26-storey concrete tower was established as the new London Stock Exchange in Throgmorton Street almost on the spot where New Jonathan's had once flourished. Opened by Queen Elizabeth in 1972, it stood as a seemingly unassailable bastion of capitalism in a climate where the City of London was often under political scrutiny and attack, and where Britain was in deep economic and industrial decline.

The early years in 'Throg Street' were good years for the practitioners in the market. While heavy industry had crumbled – and much of manufacturing industry had vanished under international competition from Europe and southeast Asia – the banks and other financial institutions that provided much of Britain's invisible exports thrived and prospered. Britain was still merchant banker to the free world, and overseas governments, corporations and individual potentates entrusted their dollars, gold and silver to financial houses in the square mile of the City. In the early 1980s more than £50 million worth of foreign currency changed hands each day in London, yielding banks and other dealers large sums in commission, making London the dominant market in foreign exchange with one third of world business.

The City was a club, as cosy and impenetrable as any of the establishments in St James's two miles away which served diplomats and the officer class. Those invited to share its mysteries at generous lunches or livery dinners sniffed an uneasy air of narrow bonhomie and patrimony. Above all it was a closed shop.

The members of the London Stock Exchange were particularly well protected. No one could buy or sell shares except through one of their member firms, most of which had been in the hands of the same family for decades. And, as a consequence of a closed shop, resembling a protection racket, investors had to pay twice for each transaction; a commission for the stockbroker and a mark-up for the stockjobber.

Commissions were fixed, in the manner of most professional fees at the time. For a broker to discount a commission, even to a friend, was as serious an offence as a doctor committing adultery with a patient or a farm worker poaching a landowner's pheasants. Stockbrokers brandished a pocket guide, published by Messrs Basil, Montgomery, Lloyd and Ward, which until 1975 set out an elaborate sliding scale of charges.

In 1950 a share valued at 15 shillings (at the rate of 20 shillings to the pound and 12 pence to the shilling) cost a purchaser 15s. 5¼d, after paying government stamp duty of 3¾d and commission of a modest 1½d. A £5 share would cost £5. 2s. 9d, with the broker getting 9d for his pains. By 1952 commission rates had gone up – to 0.75 per cent, but the 15s share still cost the saver only ¾d more at 15s 6d, while the £5 share cost him £5. 3s, with the broker getting a whole shilling instead of 9d for the trade.

Ten years later the rates were much higher at 1.25 per cent, but in the case of transactions over £2,500, the broker could, at his discretion, reduce the commission to not less than half the standard rates, provided the business was not shared with an agent, in which case the full rate had to be charged. On 14 February 1975 there was another rise – to 1.5 per cent for the first £5,000 consideration, falling to 0.625 per cent for the next £15,000. Decimalization had made calculations simpler: the £5 share now cost the investor £5.1625, of which 10 pence went in stamp duty and 6.25 pence in commission.

At these levels and with the volumes of business that were available to the limited number of stockbrokers, it was a profitable and relatively stress-free occupation. Advertising was banned, so clients were obtained through personal networking – usually over a substantial lunch, a game of cards in the first-class rail compartment on the way home, or a round of golf. The better broking firms used some of their profits to undertake detailed research into the activities of major companies, the results of which were made freely available to the investing institutions and more moneyed private customers.

The stockbroker did not have to sully his hands in direct financial bargaining with other brokers; indeed, until 1986, he was prohibited from doing so. Share trading was in the hands of stockjobbers, shrewd and resilient characters who stood or perched on stools at the elevated benches on the floor of the London Stock Exchange. Many of them had a demeanour more akin to a barrow-boy or bookmaker than to a City gent, and their daily work had many similarities. The jobbers made the market, deciding at what price they would buy or sell the shares on offer. Their profit was the difference between the buying and selling price, known as the 'jobbers' turn'.

Jobbers never dealt with the investing public, at any level. They traded only with dealers, usually junior employees of stockbroking firms, who were based on the floor of the Exchange, and who took their instructions by telephone or by sign language from colleagues standing nearby. Trading started at nine and finished at four-thirty, with an hour's break for lunch, and, at peak times, provided a colourful spectacle to visitors peering down from the gallery above. Occasionally trading would be punctuated by the ringing of a bell, signifying an announcement to the Exchange, which would usually be followed by a roar of approval or derision, a quick revision by jobbers of their prices, and another burst of trading. In day-to-day trading both dealer and jobber had to display a certain amount of guile.

Big Bang

October 1986 was the most momentous month in the long history of the London Stock Exchange – a combination of forces for change known as Big Bang. One force was the prime minister of the time, Margaret Thatcher. In her assault on trade unions' restrictive practices she determined that fixed commissions charged by stockbrokers should be abolished, and that all major financial institutions should have free and open access to the capital markets. The principal barriers between banks, merchant banks, investment institutions and stockbrokers should be broken down: all should be able to set up as one-stop financial supermarkets if they wished to. Why not allow one company to buy and sell shares for clients, raise capital for business, invest in new ventures, and trade in international securities like eurobonds?

But by far the biggest force for change was technology: the combination of hi-speed telecommunications and the microprocessor meant that international deals could be carried out anywhere. There was no need for any of the very large trades to pass through the Stock Exchange at all.

Immediately prior to Big Bang, 62 per cent of the trading in one of Britain's largest companies, ICI, was being transacted off the London Exchange, mainly in New York. A large share of the buying and selling of other major British companies had also been taking place in the United States. This trading was by no means confined to American investors, for some of the big British institutions found that dealing across the Atlantic was a better proposition. An official of the Prudential Assurance Company explained: 'When we have a significant buying programme on we check all available markets. We take the attitude that we deal wherever we can get the best price.'

Effectively the big traders had begun to bypass London, where the complicated system of brokers and jobbers was costing them much more in commission, government stamp duty and Value Added Tax.

For Sir Nicholas Goodison, chairman of the Stock Exchange, sweeping reform was the only solution. If the Stock Exchange was to compete with the giant American broking houses, it had to join them at their own game. There was no choice when competition was creaming off the top business, both in value and volume. Otherwise there would be nothing left for the old-fashioned Stock Exchange, and the jobbers would be left standing at their pitches.

Effecting the necessary changes took time and considerable resolution. It meant ending a way of life that had been a tradition for more than 100 years. Even though its members saw the system was under threat, the Stock Exchange Council had to be given a firm nudge in the direction of change by the government. This happened almost by accident. The Office of Fair Trading had argued that stockbrokers should be treated no differently from other sectors of the community – solicitors, estate agents, motor traders, soap powder manufacturers – who had been barred from fixing prices amongst each other, and were now bound to offer some semblance of competition in the market-place. When the Stock Exchange demurred, the government decided to take legal action, using the weight of the Monopolies Commission to take apart the entire rule book of the Exchange as a litany of restrictive practices. The proceedings were estimated to take five years to complete, and to cost at least £5 million in legal fees. It was, of course, like using a sledgehammer to crack a nut and an absurd way of challenging an entire trading system. As Sir Nicholas Goodison, chairman at the time, was to say later:

> It was a foolish way to study the future of a great international market. It was a matter which needed long and close study, and preferably a public examination not constrained by the requirements of litigation or the strait-jacket of court procedure. Unfortunately the government turned down the suggestion of such an examination, and we were forced into a position of defence of rules, not all of which we would necessarily wish to keep. Thus open debate became impossible because anything said could, as it were, be taken down in evidence and used in court. The case pre-empted resources, effort and thought.

It did, however, concentrate the mind of the council members of the Stock Exchange. The government was clearly in no mood to set up a Royal Commission to inquire into the Stock Exchange; Ministers saw that as a waste of time. If the legal case went on, with each side producing volumes of written evidence, as well as witnesses for examination, cross-examination and re-examination, the Stock Exchange would end up in an unwinnable situation. There would also be unfavourable publicity. And even if the Exchange won the legal battle, its joy would be short-lived, for such was the resolve of the Thatcher government to curb the restrictive power of trade unions that it could hardly spare a notorious City club, and would feel obliged to legislate to change the law.

In July 1983 the government offered Goodison a face-saver. It offered to drop the case against the Stock Exchange, if the Council would follow the example of New York in

1985 and abandon fixed commissions. It did so, and the die was cast for the biggest change since the days of the Change Alley coffee shops.

With the abolition of fixed commissions, which provided a steady and solid income, more or less indexed to the rate of inflation, many stockbrokers could not survive. Competition over commissions might be acceptable in a bull market, but when the bears emerged in strength there would be trouble. A bull is the name for the optimist who believes that prices are likely to go higher, and who charges into the market to buy; if there are enough bulls, their confidence is sufficient to push up prices, and commissions. A bear is the opposite market animal, who fears the worst, and expects a fall. When the bears run for cover, you have a bear market. For stockbrokers, a bear market generates fear, for although there are good commissions to be had when there is pronounced selling, the prices on which those commissions are based are lower, and interest dies.

From the perspective of the old-style broker, the future was grim. New technologies would force a change in the clubbish lifestyle. There would be fewer lunches at the club, or days out on the golf course. Those who wanted to survive would have to behave like Chicago futures dealers. Life would become unbearable – just like a job on the money or commodity markets, with young men and women arriving to a room full of telephones and computer terminals at 7.30 every morning, shouting at them and at each other for at least 12 hours, and leaving exhausted in the evening. This was a world where the midlife crisis came at the age of twenty-six.

And competition would be so fierce there would probably be less profit. With no fixed commissions, firms would have neither the time nor the resources to undertake company or sector research, let alone visit a firm and enjoy a steak and kidney pie in a country hotel with the chairman and managing director. Instead they would spend their days peering at monitors, and yelling down the telephone.

As for open ownership, well, the senior partners would sell out, pocket their millions, and go to live in Bermuda, whilst those left would not know who their bosses were, only that they worked for some large bank, almost certainly under foreign ownership. It was hard for them to imagine so great a change from the way they had been.

Despite their defeat over commissions, the Old Guard held out against other reforms. However on 4 June 1985 the 4,495 members of the Stock Exchange were confronted with an historic choice: to face up to the future or face the consequences of living with the past.

Two resolutions were put to the members voting on the floor of the Exchange. For chairman Goodison, whose passion for old clocks belied his modern outlook, the issue was clear. It was about 'whether or not members want to keep the bulk of the securities business in this country and in the Stock Exchange', he wrote in a letter. 'It is about keeping and strengthening the Stock Exchange as the natural market in securities.'

The first resolution, which required only a simple majority, would enable outsiders – banks, finance houses, international conglomerates, money brokers – to own up to 100 per cent of a member firm, instead of only 29.9 per cent. The second resolution required a 75 per cent majority, and proposed changes in the Stock Exchange Constitution to shift ownership of the Exchange from individual members to member firms. Plans were to be devised whereby members could sell their shares in the Exchange to newcomers. The first resolution was passed by 3,246 votes to 681, but the second failed by a very small margin, achieving 73.64 per cent instead of the required 75 per cent. For Goodison, this was a major setback, but for those who voted against it, the resolution was to prove an even greater blow.

Goodison had already warned members that to reject the proposal would be 'very serious and could cause substantial damage to the standing of the Stock Exchange', mainly because new entrants from America and elsewhere, if denied easy membership, would decide simply to bypass its activities. But he had one major card to play. Under his leadership the Stock Exchange's reputation and credibility had been high. In almost every other area of the City there had been scandal, but the Stock Exchange had retained its integrity, and had been shown to be a more effective policeman of those within its province than the Bank of England. Goodison was able to secure the Stock Exchange's right to self-regulation under the Conservative government's proposed financial services legislation, thus making it certain that those who wished to trade in British equities would want to be governed by its rules. The Exchange's Council then moved to create the new class of corporate membership effective from March 1986.

Corporate members would then each own one share, which gave them the right to take part in all of the Stock Exchange's trading activities, and to use its settlement and other facilities. But there would be no need for any corporate member to have an individual member on either its board or staff, although all those in its employ who had contact with customers would have to be 'approved persons'. Thus, those members who had voted against the Council on the second resolution in the hope of getting better terms for selling their individual shares to new conglomerate members found that these shares were virtually worthless. The biggest group in the world could join the club for only one share, negotiating the price, not with old members, but with the Stock Exchange Council.

The World's First International Exchange
No sooner had the new deal gone through and the day of Big Bang passed, relatively without incident, than Goodison achieved a major coup. As outlined earlier, one of the major threats to the London Stock Exchange was international equity trading bypassing London altogether. Even though the new rules made London less uncompetitive – and electronic dealing systems forced traders to work faster – there was still a large group of securities houses trading international stocks who saw no good reason why they should be part of the new Exchange.

They had formed themselves into ISRO, the International Securities Regulatory Organization, which, despite its grandiose title, showed very little affection for regulation. Its members traded in the stocks of about 400 of the world's major corporations for the benefit of about 80 institutions. It was an exclusive club for the big boys, who argued that since they all knew each other not many rules were needed.

Prior to Big Bang ISRO and the London Exchange were not exactly the best of friends; indeed they often traded insults. Since international equities were stocks which were traded beyond their own country boundaries, it was argued they should not be subject to rigid domestic rules. And a new class of international equity was being spawned: issues by international corporations underwritten and distributed in alien countries. The first really large issue of this kind was British Telecom; when it was floated off by the British government a large proportion of the stock was success-fully offered to institutions in North America, Europe and Japan.

Such international equity issues are organized by invest-ment banks and securities houses who offer tranches of stock directly to favoured clients without touching the stock mar-kets. Because of London's position at the centre of the world business time zone, most of this business has been conducted there. Goodison approached ISRO and suggested that sooner or later some form of ordered regulation for the conduct of global equity markets would be forced on it, if it did not form an international standard of its own; and since the London Stock Exchange offered the nearest to such a standard, why not merge with it?

From the Stock Exchange point of view the proposed deal averted the possibility of the world's financial giants setting up a competing market-place in London, and, according to Goodison, opened 'the way for a united securities market which will be a very powerful competitor for international business'.

On 12 November 1986, members of the Stock Exchange voted for the merger, and the combined body became known as the International Stock Exchange of the United Kingdom and Northern Ireland. The old guard knew there was no choice – the new Exchange was going to be dominated by foreigners, but so what? The previous changes they had approved had already allowed foreign financial houses to take over two-thirds of large British broking firms, and so domination by the likes of Citicorp, American Express, Deutsche Bank, Merrill Lynch, Nomura, and the Swiss Banking Corporation was anyway inevitable. There was also a sweetener of £10,000 for each member when they retired or reached the age of sixty.

The New Conglomerates

The establishment of giant new conglomerates that accompanied Big Bang led to an undignified scramble as City and international broking firms, banks and finance houses rushed to jump into bed with each other. So unseemly was the haste that some parted company with new-found, if expensive, friends within days rather than weeks, in a kind of financial promiscuity which must have left old faithfuls gasping for breath. One major bank bought a firm of jobbers only to find that, by the time the ink was dry on the contract, the best people had all left en masse to join a rival. Since these people had been almost the firm's only asset, the acquisition was more or less worthless. The Deputy Governor of the Bank of England put his finger on the problem:

> If key staff – and on occasions whole teams – can be offered inducements to move suddenly from one institution to another it becomes very difficult for any bank to rely on the commitment individuals will give to implementing its plans, and adds a further dimension of risk to any bank which is building its strategy largely around a few individuals' skills.

The banks and merchant banks were the predators, but they found even the very large broking firms only too willing to submit. Typical of the alliances formed was Barclays de Zoete Wedd, a merger between the investing banking side of Barclays Bank plc, the large stockbrokers, de Zoete and Bevan, and London's largest stockjobber in gilt-edged securities, Wedd, Durlacher & Mordaunt. Barclays became top dog, owning 75 per cent of the shares, but by the end of the decade had sold a big chunk of the business. Another group was Mercury Asset Management, formed by S. G. Warburg and Co., with three major broking and jobbing firms. Each of these two giants is able to issue securities, to place them with its large clientele base, and to buy and sell speculatively on its own account. MAM survived only one decade before being gobbled up by the world's largest securities business, Merrill Lynch.

All but one of Britain's top twenty broking and jobbing houses were absorbed into large new financial conglomerates. Among the leading firms, only Cazenove and Co.

remained independent. By taking this step, it benefited from both institutions and private investors seeking out brokers with no commercial link, and therefore no potential conflict of interest with a bank, an insurance company or a unit trust management company.

What were created were new megagroups able to act as bankers to a corporation, raise long-term capital for it through debt or equity, make a market in its shares, retail them to investors, and buy them as managers of discretionary funds. The question at the time was how could the public be sure that those at the marketing end of the firm were not privy to insider information, and, if they were, how could they be prevented from acting upon it? Sensitive information does not, of course, have to be in written form in a report. A nudge and a wink over lunch is a more subtle, and less detectable way of passing secrets. The official Stock Exchange answer to this problem was that 'Chinese Walls' had to be erected between the various parts of a financial services company, so that the interest of the public or investors would always be put first. Whether this has happened is still open to debate.

The arrival of the new monoliths badly upset the staid City career structure. Salaries rocketed as a game of musical chairs for all but the most mundane jobs got under way. Staffs of merchant banks and broking firms, whose only regular bright spot had previously been the annual bonus payment, suddenly found, to their wonderment, that they had taken over from soccer professionals as the group in society most likely to be able to bid up earnings without lifting their game. 'The trick,' one twenty-six-year-old woman employed by a Swiss bank told me, 'is to always appear to be in demand. If they think you are about to leave, they will offer more without you having to ask for it.'

One might have expected the level of poaching to diminish over time. But, more than ten years after Big Bang, generous offers were still being made to whole teams of analysts. One of the worst to suffer was Deutsche Morgan Grenfell, an institution formed out of an alliance between one of London's oldest firms and the powerful Deutsche Bank. In 1997, it lost its entire four-person emerging market bond team to the Japanese group, Daiwa Europe. In the same month its deputy chairman, Peter Cadbury, responsible for some of Morgan Grenfell's most important relationships management, left to become joint chairman of a large corporate finance institution.

Some of the individuals involved cut a very high profile, none more so than Nicola Horlick, mother-of-five from London, who made the headlines when she parted company with Deutsche Morgan Grenfell after being seen having lunch with senior officers from another company. It was alleged that she was planning to leave the company, for whom her team had quadrupled the value of the funds under management, a suggestion she strenuously denied. But within six months, after a series of tear-jerking stories in the tabloids about how as a woman in the City she had been 'picked on', she was leaving her £3 million home shortly after dawn each morning for a new job at DMG's deadly rivals, the French-owned Société Générale Asset Management. She was joined there by an old friend, John Richards, who had been on 'gardening leave', a euphemism for sitting at home doing nothing, after resigning as head of institutional investment management at another rival, Mercury Asset Management. Horlick's lifestyle, her £1 million a year income package, and her huge responsibilities, led to her being dubbed 'superwoman', a highly sexist remark because no one would ascribe the title 'superman' to a male with comparable responsibilities. On the other hand few would agree with Nicola Horlick's own description of herself as 'an ordinary person doing an ordinary job'.

Another high-profile defection took place in 1999 when ABN Amro, the Dutch international banking group, lost its entire top-ranking banking research team to rival Morgan Stanley. For ABN Amro it was an unhappy year, for it had already seen the head of its oils team, and its entire pharmaceuticals team walk out. ABN Amro was philosophical. 'This is just part of the natural ebb and flow of analysts,' the company said.*

Such is the new City, highly competitive with little loyalty.

Along with a move towards a super league of financial conglomerates came another switch of attitudes – an

---

Financial Times 10 September 1999.

obsession with short-term performance. It has become clear that fund managers – the men and women who manage the money in pension funds, life assurance companies and unit trusts – are no longer prepared to play safe by maintaining large holdings in giant but dull corporations. Not long ago the average institutional investor shared his portfolio between government gilt-edged securities (interest-bearing bonds) and blue-chip equities (shares in well-known companies like Unilever, BP and ICI).

Now they prefer to move their money around, terrifying corporate treasurers who watch, helpless, as large blocks of their companies' shares are traded for what seems fashion or a whim. A fund manager may desert GEC, as many did soon after Big Bang, and buy into Siemens of Germany, Microsoft of America or NTT of Japan, thereby gambling on future currency movements as well as on the future profitability of a company or market sector. Or he may buy eurobonds. And because of the risk of volatile movements in exchange or interest rates, he may protect himself by an options or futures contract (of which more later), or both. The result is that fund managers tend towards taking profits whenever they present themselves. The only goal is shareholder value. So what are shares and how are they valued?

3   Shares, Bonds and Other Forms of Paper Money

'It's paper anyway. It was paper when we started and it's paper now' – Sam Moore Walton, founder of Wal-Mart.

'When stocks go down, shoeshine goes down. It's rough' – Wall Street shoe cleaner.

'Risks are explicit, and well priced. The skills of the bookmaker have proved more reliable than those of the banker' – Anthony Harris, economist and columnist, *The Times*.

From time to time television newscasters tell us in their breathless headline style that billions of pounds – or dollars, francs or marks – have been wiped off the value of shares. To most ordinary people such stories are meaningless, as since they are inclined to believe that shares are not for them they do not take much interest. Even the minority of viewers that are economically literate may pause to ponder why BP or BT are worth hundreds of millions of dollars less today than yesterday, but then shift their attention elsewhere. The broadcasters, adopting their self-styled mission to explain, never let such stories pass without interpretation, more often than not plausible though wrong. They frequently take the opinion of a smartly dressed young market analyst, many of whom are of the type who are never slow to offer opinions, and who were once described contemptuously by a former British Chancellor of the Exchequer as 'teenage scribblers'.

Each share represents a tiny but equal percentage of a company. The actual value of a public company whose stock is listed on an exchange will always be the price of each share at any given time multiplied by the number of shares. The equation does not work the other way round. Companies are not like individuals. When applying for a mortgage the lender assesses an individual's net worth by aggregating the person's assets and deducting from that sum their liabilities. Perform the same operation with a company, and you get its net asset value – or NAV as it is known. Divide that by the number of shares and you get NAV per share. Neither figure is real value. Real value depends on day-to-day perception of the market, not accountancy.

Often this real value seems illogical, especially when share prices appear to bear little relationship to the company's sales performance, or to the profit and loss account. Employees who see those amongst their number being made redundant at a time when share prices are at an all-time high are perplexed. This perplexity can turn to anger when they see their bosses reaping large bonuses when the share value is slumping.

But this lack of logic is what makes the stock markets fascinating. There are many reasons why shares move up and down, and here are some of them, starting with the obvious:

1. **The company is doing badly.** If a company has a poor year, as did British Airways in 1999, then the share price will fall. But remember that share price always reflects perception, or at least the investors' collective view as to where the company is going. So although British Airways' profits at the start of the year were not that bad, investors felt they would slip, and the share price fell. When BA announced a loss for the second quarter of the year, these investors were proved right, but the shares did not drop further because enough people felt that chief executive Robert Ayling's strategy for recovery was the right one, though opinion was divided. Much the same happened to Marks and Spencer in the same year. M&S was once a favourite share in many people's portfolios, but fell from grace when the perception of the company changed to the view that its fashions were stale, its goods too pricey, and its buyers out of touch with the market.

2. **The company may be doing fine, but there is unease about the general direction of the economy and interest rates.** Frequently the market as a whole is unnerved by the prospects ahead. This could be because interest rates are

believed to be on the rise, or because of a variety of global and regional economic factors which affect investor sentiment. Few shares move against a very significant downward trend in global markets, such as the world stock market crash of 1987, or the Asian crash of 1998.

3. **The company has bold and strong leadership, which seems to know where it is going.** This has certainly been the case with many well-led large American companies, such as General Electric, headed by the redoubtable Jack Welch; Microsoft, controlled by Bill Gates; Michael Dell's Dell Computer, and Intel, inspired by Andy Grove. These high-profile personalities add an extra dimension to their corporations, and investors have faith in their leadership skills and management philosophies. Welch, for example, believes that GE should either be number one or number two in its sector, or out of it. Conversely a company which appears to have weak leaders who lack strategic direction will lose investor support, and shares will fall.

4. **The government may interfere with the company.** Gone are the days when many large companies were in danger of being compulsorily acquired by the state. The march of privatization has meant that governments have been busy divesting themselves of businesses. But governments love to interfere, and often pass legislation which will disadvantage some companies. Or government-appointed regulators tighten controls – and limit profits – of near-monopolies like British Telecom and British Gas. In Britain in 1999 the risk of government meddling in the affairs of the privatized rail companies depressed share prices in this sector, while providing some public-relations balm for the stoic band of aggrieved rail travellers using their services.

5. **The shares are in a sector which is trendy.** In the late nineties the sexy sector was that comprising internet stocks. Most of the companies in this sector have never turned a profit, and yet are apparently worth billions. The best example was perhaps Amazon.com, an online service for selling books at modest discounts from store prices. Although unprofitable, it achieved a market capitalization in 1999 in excess of $1.5 billion, putting it well ahead of some of the best known, most profitable companies in the world. On the eastern side of the Atlantic a curious

phenomenon was Freeserve, an internet service provider spun off by the Dixons retail chain. Although Freeserve offered an indifferent product with little to recommend it compared with the competition, its stock soared on the London stock market, and shortly after its float was worth more than its parent. And of course Dixon's own shares rose to unprecedented levels because it retained majority ownership in its prodigy.

6. **Investment gurus like certain companies.** There are a number of well-known investment gurus in the world today whose investment and speculative skills have helped them to become multi-millionaires. These men include Warren Buffet, Henry Kaufmann, George Soros, Peter Lynch and Ron Brierley. All have a strong following, and when they act in the market, it sets a trend.

7. **Competition may be so tough that profits are hard to foresee.** There is such fierce price competition in some sectors that the companies' margins are always under threat. In Britain this is true of the food supermarket sector, where well-run companies like Tesco offer safe rather than spectacular profit growth, and therefore can be unappealing to the investor looking for above average returns. Worldwide airlines fall into the same trap. There is so much capacity – seats in search of a bottom on them – that air fares are too low to produce good yields.

8. **The company has been talked up in public relations campaigns.** Many companies employ investor relations managers or public relations consultants to put a favourable spin on their activities in order to keep share prices high. A high share price – with the resultant high market capitalization – makes a company less vulnerable to takeover, and therefore leaves the executives in charge feeling more secure. It also boosts the value of their own stock options. Watch for profiles of chairmen and chief executives that are 'placed' in newspaper feature pages to enable them to talk up the company.

9. **The company may be under family control.** Families sometimes have motives which may go beyond profit. A company may be a way of life. The Dow Jones Company, which publishes the excellent *Wall Street Journal*, has been criticized by shareholders for paying more attention to style than

earnings. Family ownership tends to cause particularly severe problems in media corporations, where wilful and strange decisions are often taken. A power hungry media mogul may overpay to acquire another prestigious title, for reasons of ego as much as anything else. When Rupert Murdoch bought the *New York Post* from Dorothy Schiff it lost money, and has been leaking dollars ever since. But it was the only New York daily available, and Murdoch enjoyed owning it, even if it benefited the shareholders little. Much the same could be said of his acquisition of *The Times* in London. News Corporation is also not renowned for paying generous dividends; the Murdoch family don't need the money, which would be taxable, and prefer to continue to risk it in the business. In Australia the Fairfax family seriously mismanaged the *Sydney Morning Herald*, which should have been the prime property that it has now become. There are also problems of succession to consider in companies where a family is the principal shareholder. Many companies survive one generation, but not too many go beyond three, for there are usually too many grandchildren to fight over the spoils or the jobs.

Gilts

Gilts is short for gilt-edged securities, and these, as the name suggests, are units of a loan tranche issued by the government to fund its spending. Gilts are issued for a fixed term at a fixed rate of interest, though no one is obligated to hold them for the whole period. But like all fixed interest securities they offer the holder the security of regular interest payments, as well as repayment of the amount borrowed, at maturity.

There are three types of gilts traded. Those with five years or less to run until redemption are known as shorts; those with a redemption period of between 5 and 15 years are mediums, while longs are those stocks with a redemption date of more than 15 years.

In the United States the equivalent to gilts are bonds known as Treasuries – because they are issued by the United States Treasury. Treasuries, particularly long bonds, have been popular over the years with Japanese investors, who have taken the risk that the rate of return in dollars will be greater than the decline of the dollar against the yen.

Large corporations also issue bonds, at rates of interest which are higher than government bonds, but which are also highly secure investments. Some of these offer the option to convert the bond to equities at a favourable price. It has also become fashionable for large corporations to raise money outside the country in which they are based and in another currency. These are known as eurobonds, and almost one third of these securities are listed on the London Stock Exchange.

Another form of security is a warrant. This allows the holder the right to subscribe, at a fixed price, for shares in the company at some future date. Warrants are high-risk, and offer the holders neither dividends nor voting rights. If the holder decides not to subscribe for the underlying shares, then the paper is worthless. These, and other even more exotic securities, are known as derivatives, and the interested reader should look out one of the many specialist books devoted to them.

Riskier Paper Money

'If you are very good at market timing, you can make out like a bandit' – Donald Mesler, author of *Stock Market Options*.

Anyone unlucky enough to get on to mailing lists for financial services will have received an invitation to attend a 'three-day up-to-the-minute workshop' on 'advanced exotic options'. Many end up none the wiser about the new and sometimes rewarding opportunities offered by the markets in such areas as derivatives and options.

Many people find it difficult to come to terms with investments that are less tangible than a share in a corporation or a well-defined unit trust. Some of the new financial products that have been conceived in recent years are exotic, and many of them carry a greater degree of risk than more straightforward investments. But that is not always true. Some of these derivatives have been designed to minimise risk. You can, for example, invest in a stock market index, either by buying a

Telegraph or the *Financial Times* in Britain, or the *Wall Street Journal*. Reproduced below is part of a table from the *FT* of 14 October 1999. The underlying share is the company for whose stock an option is available, and the underlying share price is the price at the previous night's close. The exercise price is the price at which an option contract gives the holder the right to buy or sell the underlying security. The expiry date signifies when the option contract runs out, which means that if the option is not exercised by then it is invalid. And the premium is the amount per single share at which a contract may be available.

Option		CALLS				PUTS	
		Oct	Jan	–	Oct	Jan	–
ASDA	200	20	20	–	–	–	–
(*220)	220	1	1	–	–	–	–
Option		Oct	Jan	Apr	Oct	Jan	Apr
Abbey National	1100	34½	107½	139	19½	77	116½
(*1114)	1150	13	82½	111	48	101½	139
Allied Domecq	550	33	58	74½	1½	19½	29½
(*581)	600	4	31	49	22½	43	53½
Ald Dom ex	330	16	35	47	3½	18	25½
(*342)	360	2½	21½	32½	20	34	41½
Allied Zurich	700	22	60	83	4½	40	51½
(*711½)	750	3½	36½	57½	38½	65½	76½
Astra Zeneca	2800	61½	206	275	32	142	193
(*2827)	2900	18½	156	224	89½	192	241½
BAA	420	34	48	60	½	14½	21½
(*453)	460	6	26	39	12½	33	40
BAT Industries	460	17	45	57½	4½	27	43
(*472)	500	1½	27	39½	29½	49	66½
Barclays	1800	73½	186½	236½	19½	111½	164
(*1851)	1900	23	134	188	69	159	214
Bass	700	30	57½	75½	5	40½	53½
(*724)	750	5½	34	53	31	69	81½
Boots	600	40½	61	80½	1	21	33
(*639)	650	7	34	54½	17½	44½	56
British Airways	300	17½	31	41½	1	16	22
(*316)	530	2	17	27½	15½	32½	37½
BP Amoco	550	20	50	68	5½	30½	46½
(*563)	575	7	37	55	18	42	58½

Taking the example of British Airways, the chart shows that a call option to buy 1,000 shares at 300 pence in the airline any time between 14 October 1999 and January 2000 may be bought for 31 pence per share. If a longer call option period were required to buy BA at the same price, the option cost per share would be 41.5 pence. A put option for the same dates would, however, cost less – 16 pence and 22 pence per share respectively. These figures indicate that those writing the option – in other words taking the risk – expect BA shares to rise marginally rather than fall.

Writing an option contract – as distinct from buying traded options – is a job for the professionals. It reverses the risk of buying or selling an option. Essentially the writer is gambling that the option will expire worthless, and that he will have received the put or call money for taking the risk. The job is akin to that of an insurance underwriter: he charges you a premium but hopes you will never claim. And, just like the underwriter, the person writing the risk in return for a premium needs to have a thorough knowledge of the markets and companies concerned. Those that do write options are required to deposit a sum of money, called margin money, with their broker as security for the performance of their obligations.

In Britain the concept of investing in options has been slow to catch on among general investors, although it plays a major part in the lives of the professionals. There is no reason for this, other than lack of education about the markets. In the United States, where attitudes are very different, options are booming.

The Chicago Board Options Exchange is the third largest securities market in the United States, after the New York Stock Exchange and NASDAQ, and more than two-thirds of those who use it are private investors. It is helped by the attitude of the US regulatory authorities, who are strong supporters of options trading, with the Securities and Exchange Commission arguing that it significantly enhances liquidity and makes for better and more accurate markets.

Europe is catching up, though options markets are still used mostly by professional investors. In 1978 there were only two equity options markets in Europe, one in Britain and the other in Holland. Today they are either established or being set up in every advanced country.

In Britain options are traded at the only exchange with a floor, the London International Financial Futures Exchange (LIFFE), which is based under the arches of Cannon Street station, having moved there from the more august but less appropriate surroundings of the Royal Exchange, close to the famous Change Alley. LIFFE calls its trading floor area a pit, in the manner of its Chicago contemporary, and dealers work under the auction system of open outcry. It is the size of a football pitch, and those who stray into it are in danger of being kicked down.

At LIFFE they trade in options in 75 major companies – mostly Alpha stocks on SEAQ – and in the future movement of the *Financial Times* 100 Index. Orders are phoned through to the LIFFE building to operators who wear sweat-shirts identifying their firms. More than 200 firms are members, and the exchange is a hive of activity between 8.35 and 16.10 each weekday. Outside these hours the dealers, mostly young with Cockney accents, can be found in local cafés or in an adjoining health club.

But if you imagine that by buying options you are sure to win a fortune, be warned by the following remark from Stephen Figlewski, the Associate Professor of Finance at New York University:

> Small investors lose because they believe their information is better than it really is. They take positions that aren't any better than their beliefs, and their beliefs aren't any better than throwing darts.

There are other forms of share options that are much more familiar to members of the public, those that are available to employees of public companies. These are often, though not exclusively, reserved for executives, and usually allow the employee the right to buy a limited number of shares in the company for which he works once he has completed five years' service. These options are available for nothing, and the price is normally set at a discount of the price at the start of the option period. Some far-sighted employers in Britain encourage all employees to join a government-backed scheme which gives tax incentives to companies who promote a long-term saving plan with a building society or bank where the final amount saved is used to buy shares at a low-cost pre-set option price. Unless you work for a company that is on the slide, these are the best form of savings plan available, combining the benefit of regular commitments via a building society with the chance of cashing in on long-term capital appreciation. It is perhaps the only risk-free route to the stock markets. Unfortunately many companies fail to explain these schemes properly to their workforces; if they did there would be a much higher percentage of the workforce owning shares.

Futures

If trading in options sounds a little like a casino, it is dull by comparison with the activities on the futures markets. There are futures in everything – commodities like cocoa, coffee, wheat, lead, zinc and gold; meats like cattle and pork; currencies like the dollar, the yen, the deutschmark, and the pound; and of course, shares.

Buying futures is speculation, and some people make and lose millions by doing it. It requires knowledge of changing circumstances, as well as intuition as to the way events will turn out. If you think that there will be a severe frost in Brazil – or are prepared to bet that this will be so – you may buy six-month coffee futures, in the belief that by the time your coffee is delivered at the end of the period, it will be worth a lot more. Of course, there is no need for you to take delivery of the coffee at all; if the frost comes, the price of your futures contract will rise sharply, and you may sell out.

There is, of course, good reason for buying futures other than speculation. If you are a coffee wholesaler and you fear a cold snap in Brazil, you will buy futures to protect yourself, regarding the extra cost of the contract as an insurance premium. The same is true of the manufacturing industry. If you have ordered an expensive set of machine tools from Germany, due to be delivered in six months' time, you will not want to pay for them until delivery. But supposing the pound falls against the mark in the meantime? You cover yourself by buying the required amount of deutschmark futures. This process is called 'hedging'.

There are futures markets in all the major financial centres, while Chicago has assumed pre-eminence in the trading of commodities.

There has been considerable growth in bond markets, for the increase in the number of gilt-edged market makers has placed a premium on hedging contracts. For instance, a fund manager may know that in three months he will receive cash for investment in gilts, and he has picked long gilts – those maturing in 15 years' time. Rather than waiting to see what the interest rate will be at that time, he can lock into today's rate by buying LIFFE's long gilts futures contracts for delivery in three months' time. If gilt yields then decline, the investor will have to pay a higher price, but the price of the long gilts futures contracts will have risen, and the fund manager's profits will reduce the effective cost of buying the stock.

The FTSE 100 futures contract is priced by taking one-tenth of the value of the FTSE 100 Share Index published throughout each business day. It may be used by an investment manager concerned that the market will rise before he can place funds becoming available to him.

Dabbling in futures is much more risky for private investors than options. This is because of the greater leverage involved. Investing in commodity futures, in particular, has proved a fatal attraction for many speculators who have wrongly assumed that they can pit their wits against the experts: I do not recommend it. Let me give you an example of how a commodity futures contract works. Suppose coffee for delivery three months from now is trading in London at $900 per tonne. A speculator buying 10 tonnes will have coffee worth $9,000, but will have to pay only a 10 per cent deposit for a contract providing for delivery at the end of the quarter. The speculator does not, of course, take delivery. If the price goes up to $1,000 a tonne, he sells the contract and takes a handsome profit of $1,000. Although the coffee price has gone up only a little over 10 per cent, his return on capital is well over 100 per cent. But if coffee goes down to $810, he will be obliged to buy the coffee at the agreed price of $900, and then sell it again before delivery at its lower market rate. The loss would probably more than wipe out his deposit; in other words he would have lost his bet.

Many people imagine that they can follow stories in newspapers and on the wires and second guess what tropical storms or frost will do to coffee prices. They are much mistaken. The professional buyers, working for companies like Nestlé, Kenco or Maxwell House, have agents on the plantations and know exactly what the crop will be. My guess is that anyone seriously interested in trading futures will probably not be reading this book; for the newcomer or nonprofessional, trading options is probably as risky as one will want to get.

Emerging Markets

While there are exceptions to every rule, it is often the case that the less you know about a country, or a company in that country, the riskier the investment. It follows that sometimes the rewards can also be great. As stock market investments have proliferated, and new exchanges opened or old ones been revitalized, a sector that has become of considerable interest to investors prepared to take risks are the emerging markets. There are now stock markets operating in at least 60 countries worldwide.

Emerging markets split into several groups. There are those in south-east Asia, which attracted considerable interest in the mid 1990s as the Asian 'tiger' economies grew, though suffered some setback in 1998 when markets collapsed. Separated from this group, but reflecting the extraordinary size of the Indian economy, is the Bombay Stock Exchange, which in 1995 was the best performing global stock market. Indian shares have been particularly popular amongst the large Indian communities working in the Gulf.

Then there are a variety of Middle East markets. In many liquidity and lack of adequate regulation is a problem, but stock markets as varied as Beirut, Muscat and Bahrain have begun to arouse considerable interest amongst nationals, and a small amount of participation elsewhere.

Central and Eastern Europe is another emerging market sector, where investment has been stimulated by the many privatizations that have taken place although, all too often, with the result that the old communists who controlled businesses before the collapse of Comecon are the new capitalists of today.

Latin America is following the pattern of south-east Asia, and a special case is South Africa. Although the Johannesburg Stock Exchange is one of the oldest in the world, there is no doubt that the new South Africa is an emerging market with its fair share of risk and reward. So far it has chosen to go down the route of democratic capitalism. President Nelson Mandela, upon release from 27 years of incarceration, initially embraced socialism, and, upon election, opposed privatization. His team of African National Congress ministers, including the able Trevor Manuel, his minister for finance, and Thabo Mbeke, the deputy president, persuaded him to change his mind, and South Africa, despite numerous setbacks, now offers opportunities to those prepared to take some risks.

Not everybody agrees that the expansion of stock markets in developing countries will expand their economies and eradicate poverty. In the *Economic Journal* of May 1997, Ajit Singh of the University of Cambridge argued that they were more of a hindrance. Many of Singh's arguments are well worn – that stock markets are short-termist, that swings in share prices can be too volatile, and that those in emerging markets are little more than a casino. It is true that in many markets there can be a boom and bust mentality, which, at one level, raises investors' expectations beyond what is reasonable, and, at the other end of the equation, provides for despair which has little relation to the facts. Similar concerns have been raised by the billionaire investor George Soros, who has repeatedly warned that unexpected and chaotic movements of financial markets might destroy society. 'We are creating global financial markets without understanding their true nature,' warned Soros in May 1997. 'We have this false theory that markets, left to their own devices, tend towards equilibrium.'

Another argument mustered against paper wealth is that it encourages a consumer boom, which then has to be choked off by higher interest rates, depressing economic growth. This seemed to be the case with the windfall gains provided in Britain by the demutualization of some building societies and life assurers in 1996–98. So much cash was released into the market as members sold their shares that interest rates went up. In an emerging market like South Africa the same process created considerable disquiet amongst the majority black community who, of course, were not the beneficiaries of windfall gains.

In a letter to the Natal Mercury complaining that the £3.5 billion windfall from the demutualization of South African Mutual was a 'sad reflection of society's greed', Terry Crawford-Browne wrote:

> Demutualization is a ploy to enrich the financial *status quo*, so that the rich (whites) get richer and the poor (blacks) get poorer. It is a recipe for revolution. The long-term implications for the country are disastrous. Our cities are housing time bombs, ringed by shantytowns and blighted by crime. The shacks of seven million South Africans are a disgrace to a financial institution like South Africa Mutual. Cape Town urgently needs 120,000 houses. At 50,000 rand a house (about £6,500) the cost would be 6 billion rand. That is almost petty cash for the 235 billion rand institution which is so cash flush that it proposes both to pay its policyholders 29.3 billion demutualization profit and to transfer 50 billion rand out of South Africa.

These fierce words show why, in an emerging market like South Africa, share ownership and capital markets may have gathered a bad name. Against that the equity markets have financed ventures too risky for the staid commercial banks to consider. Mr Singh's own study showed that in many developing countries equity finance accounts for a greater share of company finance than in a mature economy like Britain's. It also exceeded bank finance. Countries where this was the case included Brazil, Jordan, Korea, Malaysia, Mexico, Turkey and Zimbabwe.

4   The Share Buyers

Almost everyone owns shares, either directly or through third parties investing on their behalf in pension schemes, life assurance, unit trusts, mutual funds or other pooled investments. In recent years there has been a conspicuous rise in the number of individuals who have chosen to buy and sell their own stocks, instead of or in addition to collective investments. In Britain and Europe the number of private shareholders rose sharply after the great privatizations of the eighties and nineties, and they now form a substantial portion of the pool of investors, though not the largest.

That category is reserved for institutional investors who, according to the most recent credible survey, own just over half of the £1,268 billion worth of shares in the market.*

The largest single group are insurance companies, whose holdings in 1997 were £290 billion of the £669 billion held within the institutional sector. Individuals hold about 16 per cent, at £203 billion, but this number does not count personal holdings in unit trusts, described later. Although individual shareholdings have risen in recent years, they still need to climb further to get back to the level of 1981, when 28.2 per cent of stocks were in private hands, or the immediate post-war years when two-thirds were.

Private ownership was wiped out by the disastrous nationalization programmes of successive Labour governments. Now control by the state has been replaced with control by the fund managers employed by institutions like Merrill Lynch, Prudential Assurance and Fidelity.

Most fund managers have never dirtied their hands in manufacturing industry, or hustled for business in an overseas market, or designed a robot, a machine tool, or a new building. Whether based in London, New York, Tokyo or a

---

*The actual figure is 52.7%. Study for the Office for National Statistics by Georgeson and Co. Inc., 31 December 1997.

handful of other financial centres, they wear grey suits and the introverted look of those who have spent too long staring at spreadsheets and annual reports. They take themselves, and their jobs, seriously. Hardly a working day passes when they are not meeting with directors or managers of companies in which they have invested. Although they deny they have a day-to-day influence on managers, they do sometimes step in and exert their power when things go wrong.

Because they can sack boards, determine the outcome of takeover bids, and make or break corporations, they have to exercise this power judiciously. They are courted assiduously by corporations anxious for them to maintain or increase their holdings. When Granada mounted a hostile takeover bid for the Trusthouse Forte hotel group in the mid-nineties, Rocco Forte, son of the founder of the group, Lord Forte, mounted a huge campaign to attempt to persuade the institutions not to accept the Granada offer. Granada's Jerry Robinson and his team conducted their own battle for the hearts and minds of the same groups. At the end of the day the vote was close, with one key institution, Mercury Asset Management (now Merrill Lynch), holding sufficient shares to have the casting vote. MAM's fund manager, Carol Galley, cast it in favour of Robinson, sealing the fate of a great family business, and ensuring that famous hotels like London's Grosvenor House and the King George V in Paris would lose the individual Forte touch. The unfortunate Rocco gained plenty of cash but lost his business, and had to start from scratch again. Questions have repeatedly been asked as to whether hard-headed individuals like Galley should have this kind of power, but it is hard to see an alternative that would work.

There are many who believe that the investment institutions ought to be more interventionist. When it was revealed that some of the management of British Airways had been involved in a shoddy dirty-tricks operation against competitor Virgin Atlantic, some fund-management groups complained to the airline's directors. But none of BA's institutional investors went so far as to call for changes in top management, even though there were demands in the media that senior directors should resign.

While institutional investors are united in their objective

to make money for their members, there are wide differences in strategy, and the ways and means of achieving these objectives. The job of pension funds is to invest the weekly contributions deducted from salaries of employees and usually made up by their employers. These funds have the paramount objective of providing a retirement income in old age for those who have contributed. Thus risky investments must either be avoided, or limited to a small proportion of the funds under management. If a pension fund fails to provide enough cash to meet the pledges made to employees, then employers would have to make up the difference, presumably after sacking the fund manager. The better a pension fund is managed, the lower the employer's cost. So most pension funds, including those run exclusively for the benefit of trades union members, allocate their investments across a broad spectrum, preferring a diversified portfolio to excessive concentration in one or two stocks, or venturing into speculative projects in countries with dodgy economies. Almost all pension funds have, in recent years, diversified their portfolios to include investments in the United States, Western Europe, the Far East and Pacific Basin.

Life Assurance Companies

Life assurance companies have a similar outlook. Their principal concern is to see that the premium incomes received are invested adequately to meet the eventual pay-out upon death or the end of a term. It is necessary for these huge investors to match their known obligations, calculated through actuarial tables, with investments maturing at the same time. For this reason assurance companies invest heavily in long-dated gilt-edged securities or bonds. Some governments actually insist that institutions like life assurance companies and pension funds, which so often are the beneficiaries of generous tax treatment, allocate a substantial proportion of their investments to government bonds. There is, however, a trend away from such rules. Australia, for instance, has abolished what was known as the 20/30 rule whereby for every $30 invested elsewhere, $20 had to be invested in government bonds. Japan, whose pension funds have colossal clout, has gradually been easing the restrictions which made it difficult for large sums of money to be invested in other than Japanese industry.

The absence of regulation does not stop critics of capitalism objecting strongly to privileged institutional investors failing, in their view, to use their funds in the national interest. The counter-argument, of course, is that it is the duty of pension funds and life assurance companies to do the best they can for those whose money they hold in trust – future pensioners and policy-holders – and therefore their fund managers should be unfettered by nationalistic controls.

Unit Trusts

The other set of powerful institutional investors are mutual funds, known in Britain as unit trusts, and investment trusts, and other managed funds. Trusts provide ways in which small and medium-sized investors can take an interest in equity markets without having to take the risk of buying shares in individual companies.

There are about 1,400 unit trust funds in Britain alone, managed by over 150 separate London groups for over 7 million unit holders. Total unit trust investment is around £120 billion. Some of the groups are very large. As advertisements in the Saturday papers show, there is a unit trust for everybody: there are trusts that offer the prospect of capital gain, those that offer income; some that invest only in blue-chip stocks, and those that specialize in high-risk, or 'recovery', shares. There are trusts for those who will only invest in ethical propositions. These eschew stakes in tobacco companies, for instance.

Some people believe that ethical investment will assume increasing importance as families become more concerned about health and the ecology of the planet. They are probably right, but then human nature historically has often put greed before public interest. It is very hard to gauge exactly how much money is placed into ethical investments, because not everybody who places such investment does so through an established ethical unit trust, preferring to use his or her own judgement as to what is right for them. But it does seem that the managed fund sector is growing. The Ethical Investment Research Service reports that there are at least 35 unit trusts, investment trusts or personal equity plans with ethical criteria that manage a total of £1.3 billion. That figure, for 1997, was 45 per cent up on the 1995 number.

Of course, even within the ethical funds industry, there is a debate as to what is ethical and what is not. Almost everyone would agree that to invest in a tobacco company or a company involved in animal testing should be avoided, but what about road building? Jupiter Asset Management, which runs two ethical funds, told the *Investors Chronicle* it would not invest in it; others were not so sure.

Almost all unit trust management companies, many of them owned by banks, merchant banks, or insurance companies, have specialist country funds. The most popular are those with portfolios in Western Europe, the United States, Japan and Australia, and the more stable countries of southeast Asia.

A good idea of the range available can be gained by looking at the funds managed by just one average group, Gartmore Fund Managers Ltd, headquartered in London. Gartmore operates 90 trusts in six sectors. These are British growth funds, British income funds, international funds, overseas funds, pensions strategy funds, and personal pensions funds. The 14 separate growth funds are invested in equities, but with different strategies. Some concentrate on smaller companies, and two are operated through a computer program which sets out to match the weighting of stock market indices. These so-called tracker funds will be discussed later. The international funds differ from overseas funds in that the former are totally global in nature, though split into sectors like global utilities (telecommunications, water, power and gas companies), and emerging markets. The overseas funds tend each to specialize in a region, such as the United States, Europe, and Asia, or a more specific location such as Hong Kong and China. The pensions funds are also varied by sector and region.

Each of these funds would have a fund manager, whose task is to build a portfolio which performs according to the stated objectives, and who quickly has to master his or her sector, and all the companies within it.

Most unit trust companies also offer life or pension-linked funds, which in Britain allow the investor substantial tax advantages, in that the cost of units is permitted as a tax deduction so long as the investor does not sell the units or receive any dividends until retirement age.

Another form of unit trust investment which has become popular because of its tax efficiency is the umbrella fund, which allows investors to switch units between funds, without being liable for capital gains tax on any profit on the deal. This allows both fund managers and private investors to operate efficiently in the widely fluctuating foreign exchange markets.

One of the problems with unit trusts, from an investor's point of view, is that it costs rather too much to buy them. There is usually an up-front charge of 5 per cent, plus the burden of VAT, so that quite often it may be some time before the buyer can see any improvement in the value of his portfolio. The spread between the bid and the offer price is also often large – 6 per cent or more, with some as high as 14 per cent – so your units will have to rise appreciably before you can sell them at profit. And the more you switch the more it costs. There are widespread differences in the performances of the various funds, a fact which often seems to escape much public attention.

In the five years to August 1999, £1,000 invested in Aberdeen Technology, a fund managed from Scotland and concentrating on technology stocks, rose fivefold to £5,095. Another top performer over the same five-year period was Fidelity American, up fourfold to £4,175. Over a shorter three year period Fidelity was top performer, rising to £3,067. At the bottom end of the scale over five years was a South African entrant to the British unit trust scene, Old Mutual, whose Thailand Accumulator Fund had accumulated nothing. It bombed, and anyone who had put £1,000 in this had only £388 of their investment left. Over a ten-year period the booby prize went to the venerable Barclays Bank, whose Japan Fund fell by 50 per cent over this period to the consternation of those who believed that investments in the land of the rising sun would never set.*

League tables of performance published in the weekend broadsheets make interesting reading. Of course these tables are about as useful as a league table in professional football. Just because you are top one month does not mean you will stay there. But just as Manchester United is usually to be found in the top tier of British football clubs, so the best funds have a consistency about them. The truth is that if you have £10,000 to invest in a fixed-interest unit trust, you will have to pay around £750 in fees, plus annual management charges. Invest in a good income-producing blue-chip company or utility via the Internet, and the most you will be charged is £100, and there will be some upside capital gains prospects.

Investment Trusts

Often confused with unit trusts, but different in concept, are investment trusts. Like unit trusts, investment trusts allow the smaller private investor to benefit from having a stake in a large portfolio of widely spread shares, both by sector and by region. But there the similarity ends. Investment trusts are public companies like any other and their shares are traded on the stock markets.

Instead of making motor cars, running hotels, or operating department stores, an investment trust company exists purely and simply to buy and sell shares in other companies, both for short-term speculative gain and long-term capital growth. Those who manage investment trusts are full-time executives responsible to a board of directors, and they buy and sell shares on the world's stock exchanges, exercising their judgement as to what will be a profitable investment. Just like any other public company, they make profits and incur losses, and pay dividends to shareholders. Because their companies have assets, investment trust executives can borrow against those assets, and are able to take both a long- and a short-term view of the money entrusted to them.

---

*Financial Times. 29 August 1999 from Lipper Analytical.

Capital gains on share trading are not distributed in cash but used to build up portfolios and, through the generosity of the Treasury, escape taxation. This means that the fund manager can realize the profits on the trust's investment at the most opportune time. Trusts can also offset their management charges against tax. Investment trusts have about £50 billion under management with 250,000 investors.

Investment trusts are cheaper to invest in than unit trusts. As stated earlier, for every £1,000 invested in unit trusts, it costs around £50 in an initial management charge. The same amount used to purchase shares in an investment trust would incur less than £30 in stockbroker's commission and government stamp duty. Unit trust managers also charge an annual fee of between 0.75 to 1.0 per cent for looking after their trusts; investment trust management charges are much lower.

Unlike individual investors, investment trust portfolio managers can take profits without paying tax, and move in and out of companies paying only dealing charges. There is also a very wide choice of funds across many markets and sectors.

So why do average investors not flock to investment trusts? The answer is hype. Unit trusts are prolific advertisers in the financial press, and therefore get much more than their fair share of space in the editorial columns that fill the empty space. By contrast, investment trusts are restricted by law in their advertising, and get comparatively little press attention. The serious newspapers provide free space to unit trusts to publicize their prices, acknowledging it a public service to do so, but provide only limited price information on investment trusts.

Moreover unit trusts are, like most life assurance products, sold by middle-men – insurance brokers, financial advisers, even accountants and solicitors. They receive a handsome commission from this form of activity, most of it up-front. With the exception of investment trust savings schemes, there is no commission for intermediaries on investment trusts, so, for the most part, they do not recommend them. The 350 or so investment trusts in Britain deserve a place in everyone's savings portfolio, and, in many cases, offer a better return than the average with-profits policy.

Another important difference, seldom understood, between investment trusts and unit trusts is that the latter tend to be priced according to their net asset value. Investment trusts, like other equities, are valued according to what the market thinks they are worth, which is more often than not below the value of their assets. The discount to NAV at the time of writing was 10 per cent, and reflects a recognition that disposing of assets costs real money, but it also reflects the market's perception of the business and the economic environment. The result is that something can be built into an investment trust's share price for future prospects. This does not happen for a unit trust.

Managed Funds

The final group of large institutional investors is different again. These are professional fund management groups, which manage, at their own discretion, the money of others, both individuals and companies. Here again there are similarities with previous groups.

At one end of the scale, there are large securities houses, which take in funds from individuals who either cannot be bothered or feel they lack the expertise to watch the market. These individuals, who range from pensioners in Worthing or Westchester County to wealthy Arabs in Dubai, entrust sums of money – the minimum is usually at least £50,000 – to fund managers who manage their portfolio, and keep them posted, through a quarterly or half-yearly report, as to what they have done with it. Only rarely would a fund manager consult a client about the purchase or sale of an investment, though most of them are receptive to suggestions. Many broking firms' fund management teams invest in unit trusts and investment trusts, and some have portfolios that stipulate these as a limitation.

Some broking houses charge for this service; others rely for income on the commission obtained through sale and purchase of shares, or from a percentage paid to them by unit trusts. This itself can lead to conflict of interest. Those brokers that leave an investment undisturbed are obviously going to benefit less than those who are constantly trading their customer's portfolio, and on many occasions there is much to be said for sticking with the status quo. At the other end of the financial scale are the large fund management groups, often a major branch or department of a well-known merchant bank. The principle is the same as with small port- folio management by brokers, but their clients are usually rich individuals, and other very large clients for whom they also act as investment bankers.

The funds under their stewardship are usually measured in billions. For instance, in 1985 Baring Brothers and Co. Ltd managed funds of more than £2,500 million, just over half of it in Britain, with clients as diverse as Bowater Corporation, London Transport and London University. Barings was to lose much of its investments through the on-screen adven- tures of its rogue trader, Nick Leeson, whose speculation cost this famous London banking family their company, which had to be saved by the Dutch group ING. Leeson was arrested for criminal fraud, and imprisoned in Singapore's Changi jail for several years.

Flemings Investment Management Ltd, with £5,800 mil- lion of clients' money to invest, managed to avoid these pit- falls, and the money it manages includes some of the funds of the Royal National Lifeboat Institution, IBM, Dow Chemical, and Whitbread. Recently Flemings have pushed hard with some success to manage the vast pool of money in the Japanese pension funds. Other big fund managers include GT Management, with the BBC as a client, Hambros Investment Management, Hill Samuel, Lazard Securities, Montague Investment Management, UBS, J. Henry Schroder Wagg and Co., N. M. Rothschild Asset Management Ltd, and Mercury Asset Management.

For all of these groups private client management means a lot more than sitting in a City office, reading research reports, and studying the prices on the electronic monitors. The good fund manager needs to have excellent judgement, the speed of decision-making of a track bookmaker, an ability to size up a balance sheet in minutes, the nose for news of a good newspaper editor, and an eye on the main chance.

With intense competition, both to sell and to perform, and round-the-world trading, the active fund manager can only grow old in the job if he or she is prepared to put work above everything. It is a long way from the days when the investment manager of the Prudential would make his way back to his office from a lunch at a West End club to place an investment of £1 million in the British Motor Corporation.

Corporate Bond Funds

Corporate bonds are a very good form of investment for those who wish to play safe, but try and get a better return than available from government bonds, known in Britain as gilt-edged securities. Corporate bonds are to companies what gilts are to Whitehall – interest-bearing loans which normally have a fixed pay-back date. They are, if you like, an IOU that can be bought and sold on the Stock Exchange. Unlike government bonds, however, they have some interesting conversion opportunities. For instance large corporations often offer bonds with a pay-back date five years on, but with the opportunity to exchange the bond for shares in the corporation instead of pay-back. These are known as convertibles, and their prices are more volatile because their performance is related to that of the share price of the company concerned.

While it is possible for individuals to buy corporate bonds, they are usually sold in large tranches, so they are mostly acquired by institutional investors. However corporate bonds are used as investment vehicles by a large number of income-based unit trusts and investment trusts, and this is perhaps the best route for individual savers who like the idea of them.

There are low-risk corporate bond funds, usually called income funds, and those that carry a greater risk, and wear the nomenclature of high-yield funds. These buy bonds from blue-chip corporations but mix them with issues from other companies more vulnerable to bad times, and therefore more likely to default. It is unlikely fund managers would go into junk bonds discussed later, because they are very high risk. But, by the nature of things, a major German motor manufacturer like BMW is less likely to collapse than a South African finance company, although both will be reasonably safe. Most of the corporations likely to issue bonds are subjected to thorough health checks by the two great world ratings agencies, Moodies and Standard and Poor. They grade a company's financial health by a star system. Triple A is at the top, triple C is fairly risky. Both these agencies also rate country's debts – or the chances of creditors being repaid – as well.

In Britain the risk of defaults by corporate bond issuers has not been great, and those considering investing in a fund should always ask for a list of the companies in which it holds bonds. Remember, though, that the risk is not just default. Another risk is that general interest rates could go up sharply, making the return on the corporate bond unattractive. This would lead to a fall in the tradable value of the bond. Generally, though, corporate bonds are attractive, providing investors with an income yield of about half as much again as deposits.

Tracker Funds

Tracker funds are a relatively new concept, and have gathered a large following. The idea is simple enough: the creation of a unit trust or investment trust company which tracks a popular index such as the FTSE 100. This index reflects the hour-by-hour fortunes of the 100 major companies in Britain, weighted by size. As a company grows so a movement in its shares carries greater weight in the formation of the index. If it slumps, then it may drop out of the index altogether. This means inevitably that movements in giants like BP-Amoco and British Telecom have considerable impact on the FTSE 100, and some believe that a better yardstick of the nation's health is the more widely and evenly spread FTSE 500.

The aim of the fund manager is to buy and sell stocks in the index in exactly the proportion in which they sit, so that his fund produces an identical performance to the index. Since so many unit trusts badly underperform the index, a tracker fund is a good way of ensuring you do not get left behind.

Constructing an equity portfolio to track any given index is not as easy as it sounds. The obvious way of doing it is to invest in all the stocks in the index at the same weightings as the index, and then adjust the portfolio whenever it changes. This is known as full-replication. But the constant adjustments that have to be made involve considerable cost, and such a scheme is expensive to administer. A number of computer programs have been generated which will achieve roughly the same result, however. Once purchased, these will allow fund managers to sleep soundly confident that they have not made major errors of judgement. This technique is called optimization, and creates a sample portfolio from a stock market index which bears the characteristics of the index itself. Developed by a number of academics at Berkeley University in California while they were investigating the components of risk in equity portfolios, the Barra program is used extensively by Bankers Trust in the United States, and has been adapted for use with the FTSE index in London by Barclays, County Natwest, and the United Bank of Kuwait. It is estimated that an optimized portfolio will track an index accurately at a value as low as £500,000, and therefore is a considerable attraction to institutions and pension fund trustees.

It is, of course, possible for an individual investor to put money into a tracker or indexed fund, but he faces the same kind of additional charges imposed for unit trusts. The more sophisticated private investor can buy computer programs to guide him in establishing his own indexed portfolio, but this has two disadvantages. Firstly, you need to be prepared to invest a substantial amount of your capital in a variety of stocks in order to make it financially worthwhile. Secondly, it removes most of the fun from investing. Like the punter slipping £50 on a horse in the Grand National, the small investor aims to beat the performance of market indices, not match them.

Tracking the index would not be possible without high-speed supercomputers, which is why the concept has only recently been established. The funds are popular with investors because both in Britain and the United States the eighties and nineties represented a fairly consistent bull market, apart from the setbacks in 1987 and 1997. If the indices had fallen for more than a few months, support for tracker funds might have ebbed away.

Up to the end of the millennium, though, research found that funds that were 'actively managed' – in other words run by a manager and his team making judgements on the state of companies in which they invested – were outperformed by 'passively managed' tracker funds.*

The research showed that over a ten-year period barely one in five active funds kept pace with the FT All-Share Index, which tracks more than 900 companies. Similarly, statistics from Standard and Poor's Micropal showed that the average FTSE 100 tracker unit trust turned £1,000 into £1,718 in the three years to 1999; by contrast the average actively managed fund produced only £1,274.

Yet at the time of writing concerns are being expressed that these tracker funds may become the victims of their own success. Consider this. Money put into tracker funds is automatically invested in the companies in the index being tracked; as we have seen the greatest share goes to the biggest companies. The effect of this is to drive their share prices up, which, in turn, pushes the index up, thus encouraging more people to join the bandwagon. This is the recipe for a crash. An overheated bull market inevitably leads to a fall, or, at best, a correction, and then the traffic starts moving the other way.

Curiously the European Commission, in a move designed to protect investors, has increased the risks. In 1998 it decided that tracker funds could invest as much as 35 per cent of their funds in a single stock, compared with a limit of 10 per cent on other managed funds. Commenting on this EC proposal, Philip Warland, director-general of the Association of Unit Trust and Investment Managers said: 'One of the safety features of investment funds is that they spread your money over a wide range of shares. This ludicrous proposal blows that concept right out of the water'.†

There are some who argue that trackers are guaranteed to underperform the index because of charges. Of the 19 funds tracking the FTSE in Britain, ten charge an initial fee – a large 6 per cent in the case of Lloyds TSB, with Govett levying 5.5 per cent and Barclays, Equitable and GA all taking 5 per

*HSBC Asset Management, *Daily Telegraph*, 12 June 1998.
†*Sunday Times*, 5 September 1999.

cent. For the All-Share, Eagle Star is the most expensive with 6 per cent, while Morgan Grenfell and Royal & SunAlliance charge 1 percentage point less.

Annual fees also vary, from a very reasonable 0.25 per cent for Scottish Widows' UK All-Share tracker to an extortionate 2 per cent on Legal & General's UK Stock Market, which tracks the FTSE. That is higher than most actively managed funds, which usually charge no more than 1.5 per cent. Indeed, many charge much less.

The Fund of Funds

Another concept is the fund of funds, designed to minimize risk for the small investor and to remove him one further stage away from direct purchases of shares. Instead of having to pick and choose between many hundreds of unit trusts, the investor could buy units in a master fund, which in turn would buy units in one or more of its subsidiary funds. From the point of view of someone with a small amount of capital to invest – but no clear idea if and when to move out of a British equity trust and into a Japanese, German or American one – the fund of funds seems no bad idea. Let someone else do the worrying and save yourself the expense of having a stockbroker to manage a portfolio of unit trusts.

Like most bright ideas, the notion was not a new one. The fund of funds first obtained notoriety as a promotion in 1962 of the international investment swindler Bernie Cornfeld, whose misdeeds are well spelt out in a brilliant book *Do You Sincerely Want To Be Rich?* by Charles Raw, Bruce Page and Godfrey Hodgson. This cautionary tale should be required reading both for investors and all those involved in the financial services industry. As the authors say:

The salesman's rationale for the Fund of Funds was an unusually owlish piece of nonsense – one of those things that sounds impressive until you really think it through. Mutual funds, and all investment concerns, are sold on the proposition that the ordinary man needs investment advisers to make choices for him. The Fund of Funds went further and suggested that the ordinary man now needed professionals to choose the professionals who would make the choices. The Fund of Funds would take your money, and invest it in other mutual funds – but only in those whose values were rising most rapidly.

A lawyer from the US Securities and Exchange Commission exploded the Fund of Funds argument succinctly:

> If funds of funds are permitted to proliferate, how would an investor decide among the many companies seeking his investment dollar? Would he not need a fund of funds of funds to make this decision?

Cornfeld's Fund of Funds run by his Investors Overseas Services and given the hard-sell by thousands of salesmen calling themselves 'financial counsellors', gathered in $100 million of people's savings within two years of its launch. The customer's money was transferred immediately into separate proprietary funds, for a brokerage fee which was pocketed by IOS. For the privilege of investing at all, the customer had to pay what has become known as a 'front-end load', much of which was used to pay a commission to the salesman who persuaded him to part with his money in the first place. For every $3,000 invested in Cornfeld's Fund of Funds, $540 vanished immediately in fees. A further 10 per cent of any income generated also went in fees, as did 10 per cent of any capital gain. According to Raw, Page and Hodgson an investor had to wait six years before he could even get his money out without loss. An investigation found that money which was supposed to be held on trust for customers was being used for the benefit of IOS itself, its directors, employees and friends; and that the IOS sales force engaged in illegal currency transactions on a major scale, and constantly misrepresented the investment performance of its largest fund.

The shockwaves that surrounded the fall of IOS were such that the British government introduced strict new rules. An approved fund of funds is restricted in its investments to its manager's own unit trusts, in total contrast with the United States where master funds may invest in anything but their own in-house trusts. A new fund of funds must also be in a group holding at least four subsidiary trusts and not more than 50 per cent of assets can be invested in any one of them.

These restrictions have narrowed the options, but one area where the fund of funds concept has continued to flourish is in investment trusts. There are several investment trusts whose *raison d'être* is to take shareholdings in other investment trusts. Instead of having to pick stocks for income or performance, a fund of funds unit or investment trust, such as Quilter's Growth IT, can pick off the best-performing and cheapest trusts, and buy and sell at discount prices.

5   Private Shareholders

'Have I made thee more profits than other princes can' – Prospero in *The Tempest*, Act I, scene ii.

'The power to make money is a gift of God' – John D. Rockefeller.

'What a wonderful time it is to be a boss of a big company. Money pours into your lap' – *The Economist*, August 1999.

Some private shareholders are in the *Forbes* magazine list of the world's richest people, and their wealth has been accumulated and grown through shares. Whereas Bill Gates and Rupert Murdoch became billionaires by building their own businesses producing goods and services, the likes of George Soros, Warren Buffett and Ron Brierley made their money by trading paper.

But amongst *Forbes'* richest people there are comparatively few traders. You find wealth through share ownership spread much deeper in society. At the start of a new century, most families in the world's industrial societies are enjoying reasonable prosperity, while many millions in the poorest nations struggle to stay alive. There is nothing new in this. What is new is the emergence of two small but high-profile groups in society that form part of the super-rich. These are people who have very considerable paper wealth that may or may not over time translate into real wealth.

The first of these fortunate groups are the high-profile executive directors and managers of major corporations. Almost all of them expect to receive considerably in excess of their agreed annual salaries, and in most cases this is achieved through the issue to them of free executive share options in the company for which they work. Though these may not be the 'gift from God' imagined by Rockefeller, they often provide a one-way bet to considerable wealth.

The stories in the newspapers about exalted earnings for chairmen and chief executives – or multi-million-pound pay-offs when they are forced out or 'retired due to ill health – usually fail to report that share options are now an important ingredient of any managers' employment package. The theory is simple: the better the company does, the more the manager gets. And the better the long-term reward, the less likely he or she will be to resign to join up with a competitor.

These kinds of share options are not to be confused with those you can buy and sell on the markets, which are discussed elsewhere. They are awarded by the employing corporation, and those lucky enough to be given them get a certificate entitling them to buy up to a specified number of the company's shares at an agreed price after an agreed length of time. Normally, but not necessarily, the price is set close to today's price, and the right to exercise the option kicks in after a period of between three to five years. If, during that time, the price falls, the options are worthless, and are not exercised. The executive gains nothing, but has lost nothing. If the shares rise sharply, there is a handsome paper profit, and tax is not normally payable on the capital gain until the shares are sold. So if you live in a country where there are capital gains taxes and you do not need the money, you can hold the shares until you have moved to a tax haven, or until you reach retirement age and pay lower taxes. Or you can sell a sufficient number each year to stay within the limit of disposals without facing a tax liability.

Thus executive share options can be a nice little earner, even if you are not responsible for the success of the company. Take the case of a senior executive in Pearson receiving 10,000 share options at the start of the 1990s, with the right to exercise them any time between 1995 and 2000. In 1990 the shares languished around the £2 mark, partly because the British market was still recovering from the 1987–88 crash and also because the company's management at the time was regarded as limp and lacking ambition. By 1998 the old management had gone, and a lively American, Marjorie Scardino, was brought in to refocus the company, whose shares had come out of the doldrums and risen to around the £6 mark. Mrs Scardino pledged to double shareholder value, and by 1999 had done better than that, with a valuation above £13. The executive with the 10,000 1990s options could exercise his rights and increase his wealth by £110,000.

While the use of executive share options in senior management compensation has grown in Britain, their significance is small when compared to what has happened in the United States, where awards have grown to astonishing levels. Since America tends to set the trend in management rewards, it may be expected the practice will become universal. According to an executive compensation company, Pearl Meyer and Partners, the 200 biggest United States companies had granted shares and share options worth about $1.1 trillion by 1998 – that is over 13 per cent of corporate equity. Fifteen of these companies have committed a quarter of their equity to such schemes. They include household-name firms like Merrill Lynch and Apple Computer. The same firm named some high-profile individuals who had made large gains on exercising options: Jack Welch of General Electric, $31.8 million; Tony O'Reilly of Heinz, $34.8 million; Andy Grove of Intel, $49 million; and Sandy Weill of Travelers $220 million.

The 'feel good' factor that these men must experience is not necessarily shared by all of those who have to get out of bed each morning to go to work for them, especially as it appears that real average earnings have fallen in the United States during the period of these grandees' enrichment. Welch, for example, is not nicknamed 'neutron Jack' for nothing, and at least part of the success at GE for which he has undoubtedly been responsible has been ruthless cost-cutting. But one of the yardsticks of success in business is to grow wealth using a minimum of resources, and dynamism in leadership is essential. The strongest argument mustered for executive share options is that if top managers were to be paid and treated like public servants they would behave like them; far better to encourage entrepreneurship by allowing them to own a sufficiently large piece of the pie to energize them into thinking like an owner.

I have already mentioned one potential problem: in a rising market the major beneficiaries may turn out to be yesterday's men. But this may not be the only case where the link between generous share options and individual executive performance is tenuous. There are major and credible reasons for the buoyancy of the American economy during the nineties that have nothing to do with corporate management. The most obvious is America's growing dominance in information technology, trouncing the argument that the United States would lose out to Japan.

The spectacular growth of information superhighways is down to brilliant innovations from Silicon Valley and a sympathetic and sensible White House. Another factor has been sound economic management by the Federal Reserve Board and the United States Treasury, both public bodies, which have allowed interest rates to fall to low levels. Those who would like to read more on this should look at a study by the economist Kevin Murphy, who has found 'surprisingly little direct evidence that higher pay-performance sensitivities lead to higher stock performance'.*

Another concern is that the incentives on offer from share options may be so great as to encourage top managers into policies that may not be in the company's long-term best interests. Cutting costs goes straight to the bottom line, thereby improving immediate performance, but it may handicap the opportunities for growth if there are not sufficient trained and skilled workers when you need them. Measures designed to build short-term share value can demoralize employees and damage service levels, as evidenced by British Airways' recent experience.

A more sinister suggestion is that chief executives are more likely to become predatory in acquiring rival corporations because of the share benefits that will accrue to them if they can swallow another large company and downsize it. The fact that their corporation may have to borrow heavily to do this is overlooked or even ignored. Against this it is argued that a motivated chief executive is less likely to go in for wasteful corporate extravagances if his reward package depends on shareholder value, and certainly some leaders make a point of practising frugality in headquarters build-

---

*'Executive Compensation', by Kevin Murphy in *A Handbook of Labour Economics*, edited by Orley Ashenfelter and David Card. North-Holland, 1998.

ings and corporate travel. Others, however, do not, and still display a lust for the trappings of power. There seems to be no clear pattern.

One curious aspect of executive share options – and an attraction for boards using them as incentives – is that in many countries they do not end up as a cost on company balance sheets. In America there were moves to do this, but corporate bosses mounted a furious lobby and defeated it. Had they done so corporate profits would not have been what they were, and perhaps share prices might not have risen so much. According to a London research company, Smithers and Co, quoted by the *Economist*, leaving out options from the balance sheet means US companies issuing them have understated profits by a half.[*]

The famous global investor, Warren Buffett, had this to say about this curious practice in the annual report of his company, Berkshire Hathaway:

> Accounting principles offer management a choice: pay employees one way and count the cost, or pay them in another form and ignore the cost. If options aren't a form of compensation, what are they? If compensation isn't an expense, what is it? And, if expenses shouldn't go into the calculation of earnings, where in the world should they go?[†]

He has a point.

Over recent years some of the spoils enjoyed by the heavy rollers have passed down the line to lesser fry. Some City firms have provided share options to all staff, and at the time of writing a group of secretaries were due each to pocket £200,000 as a five year scheme matured.[††]

Perhaps the most lucrative example of company share generosity is Microsoft, which from its early days has had a policy of offering share packages in exchange for lower salaries. In 1996 the shares rose 90-fold, and this astonishing increase made many employees very rich. A more modest scheme came from the ASDA supermarket chain, but it is one of the largest. It has over 26,000 members.

---

[*]The *Economist*, 7 August 1999.
[†]Berkshire Hathaway annual report, 1998.
[††]The *Guardian*, 7 June 1999.

Right at the other end of the scale are less well off individuals. I knew of an old man who lived extremely modestly in a caravan in the small Norfolk market town of Fakenham. By appearance he was relatively poor, as the district reporter for the local paper. But each day he bought and studied the *Financial Times*, and spent half an hour on the phone to his broker buying and selling shares. By the time he had retired from the *Eastern Daily Press* he had made more money from the stockmarket than from his modest pay as a newsman.

Many small shareholders belong to investment clubs. There are now more than 3,700 share clubs in Britain and the number is growing by more than 100 a month. These groups meet regularly to pool their cash and invest in shares they believe will perform well. An estimated six out of 10 club members have never bought shares before. An average UK investment club has 14 members and meets once a month, usually in the convivial atmosphere of a local pub.

I remember spending one wintry evening in the Conservative Club at West Houghton, an unpretentious Lancashire village in the drab industrial belt between Liverpool and Manchester. A group of women, two of them the wives of packers at a nearby baked-bean factory, were discussing the price of British Telecom shares. All had modest holdings, following the government's decision to sell off three billion shares in British Telecommunications plc to the public. The women agreed that they planned to hold on to their shares, even though they could sell out at a tidy profit. There was no doubt they had become addicted to share ownership. Since the British Telecom issue three of them had bought other shares. Said one: 'I have bought Marks & Spencer; I bought Rank Organisation and sold them again, and I am buying Dobson Park, because I think that will benefit from the end of the miners' strike.' 'I watch the prices every morning in the *Daily Mail*,' said another, 'and sometimes I keep a watch on them through the day on teletext.' Neither the women nor their families had ever had shares before. 'I did not really know how to go about it; I did not know a reputable stockbroker, or how to go about finding one, and I certainly did not know the bank would do it. It was a matter of ignorance, really.'

Share clubs seem particularly popular in the North of

England. In Leeds the Brunswick Investment Club has been going for 40 years, taking its name from Brunswick Terrace in the city, which resembled the Coronation Street of the Granada Television soap opera of the same name, but which has now been demolished. Initially it held its meetings in members' houses, but now gathers monthly in a social club with a bar. Unlike West Houghton, Brunswick is all-male, and, astonishingly, has a waiting list. Its members include a large number of retired people – mostly bank managers and clerks, accountants, civil servants, solicitors, policemen, computer salesmen and butchers.

In 1999 the chairman claimed that the club's portfolio had managed to keep pace with the FTSE 100 index over the previous 10 to 15 years.*

That year was the club's most successful in history, with a capital gain of £12,000 on share sales of £39,000, a return of almost 31 per cent. The size of the portfolio in 1999 was about £72,000, divided between about 20 holdings, and at their monthly meetings members normally agree to sell a holding and buy another one. Members do their homework on companies that interest them, and present the case for investment to the monthly meeting. If a decision to sell is not unanimous, then a vote is taken and requires a two-thirds majority based on the number of units owned in the portfolio.

The experience of West Houghton, Brunswick and many other places confirms that a vein of popular capitalism exists to be tapped in Britain. Yet it is unlikely that the burst of interest in share ownership, particularly among the working classes, would have come about if the British Telecom float had not taken place, with its hype, touring road shows, television campaign and gimmicks like bonus shares and vouchers to help pay the phone bills.

Daily Telegraph, 4 September 1999.

6   How Shares are Bought

Each morning as dawn breaks over the City of London, a square mile of grey stone and cement built on north Thames mud flats and bordered by the Tower of London to the east and the Law Courts to the west, there is an early rush hour, which starts and finishes long before the commuter trains empty their cargo of long-faced office workers. It happens quickly as new shiny cars – Mercedes, BMWs, Porsches, Saabs, Jaguars and Lexuses – are driven, tyres squealing, into some of the world's most expensive car parks. Many of the young men and women striding through the Italian-marbled entrance halls of securities houses have flushed faces and carry sports bags, evidence of a 30-minute workout in a nearby gymnasium while most Britons are still in their beds.

Upstairs, in a conference room with clocks showing the London time at seven o'clock, Tokyo at three in the afternoon, and New York at two in the morning, there is already a buzz of activity, and intense concentration. The pre-trade meeting is about to get underway. The morning newspapers have already been discarded as out-of-date; a television news channel carrying financial news flickers in the background, but over the fresh coffee and orange juice the emphasis of the dialogue among the two dozen present is on the tasks immediately ahead. A senior member of the company discusses developments in Asian markets over the phone with a colleague in Tokyo, occasionally turning up the volume on the speaker so everyone can hear. 'You are sure it's a new trend: they're not following Wall Street?' he asks. 'No, but they might be ramping that particular stock again,' comes back the answer.

A director calls the meeting to order, and bids a younger colleague to speak. 'We've got a council meeting of the Bundesbank this morning, the US trade figures, and results from British Airways and Honkers and Shankers [The Hong Kong and Shanghai Bank]. Plus a whole series of other numbers, and you've seen the Dun and Bradstreet survey which shows things might be overheating.' There is a brief discussion about the US money supply figures, and it is generally agreed that Wall Street traders the night before had already anticipated them. The company's specialist analyst on airline and transportation stocks then enters the room, carrying a sheaf of papers, which he distributes to those present. 'I think BA might surprise us,' he says. 'It's tough-going out there but they have really taken the axe to their costs.' 'Yeah, but what about the long term?' asks a young dealer with blue-striped shirt and dark blue braces. 'They've got a fight on their hands on the Atlantic, and an ageing fleet of planes.'

The discussion continues for a few minutes in similar vein, half earnest, half jousting, as the market makers – the men and women who have to set the prices at which the securities house will trade shares – challenge the seemingly unassailable logic of the analysts. Analysts, some of them trained in accountancy, some of them investment specialists, a few of them former financial journalists, are steeped in knowledge of the companies in the sectors in which they specialize. Whereas a market maker has to make a split-second judgement on the value of a stock – often reacting to a news report – an analyst usually has the time to pore over company reports and other published information, talk to company chairmen and finance directors, compare their views with those of rival executives, and even visit factories and other operations.

'I'll bet you a bottle of squiff that BA falls by more than five pence,' blue-braces offers as a parting shot, as the discussion moves on to results just announced from Hong Kong and Shanghai, showing profits sharply up. 'It might be time to look at bank stocks again,' comes a comment from a woman in another group in the corner of the room. She and her group form part of the other key element of the modern sharebroking house – the equity salesmen.

Their job is to get more business moving through the trading desks by persuading clients – many of them large investing institutions like life assurance companies, pension funds and unit trusts – to buy blocks of shares in the market. Some of these shares might already be in the possession of the securities house as a result of it being appointed to handle a rights issue. Others may have been acquired in a trading operation; some might have to be bought and sold on. Equally, an equity salesman may have a client who is interested in a particular share. He will walk over to the dealing desk, and ask a market maker how much it would cost to get hold of them.

Well before eight o'clock the meeting is over, and it is time to get to work. The equity salesmen go out to their desks and make a list of potential clients they will approach by phone. The analysts retreat behind glass partitions to paper-strewn work stations, and contemplate their next reports. And the market makers are busy at their terminals, keying in the prices to tell their counterparts across the world at what price they are prepared to deal. By eight thirty the atmosphere is like a television portrayal of the newsroom of a major newspaper, but a trifle more tense, with more fever and more bustle. Most people appear to be on the telephone, their fitful but fleeting dialogues always punctuated by taps at a keyboard, which reveal an array of coloured numbers on the bank of computer screens that dominate their desks.

Every few minutes someone gets up from his high-back swivel chair and shouts a message – or, plastic coffee beaker in hand, wanders across the floor to talk with a colleague. For the most part these dialogues are friendly and unobtrusive, but the occasional sharp-edged rejoinder reminds the observer that this is a place where serious money is at stake.

My description is of the equities floor of one of London's largest securities houses, where each working day tens of millions of pounds' worth of shares change hands. Most trading floors look the same. Large stakes in major companies are bought and sold, small allotments in privatization issues are traded, money is won or lost.

Down on the floor, on the central desk, the lead salesman touches the flickering light on his telephone panel that indicates a call is waiting, picks up the phone, and rests one foot on a drawer of his desk. The caller is a fund manager from one of Britain's largest life assurance companies. He is looking to pick up a million shares in one of the big breweries. The salesman keys into his computer the first three letters of the company's name, and the screen reveals to him that the price of the stock is higher than it has been for several weeks.

But it also shows that the posted price is only available for the purchase of 50,000 shares or less. Buying a block twenty times that size could be difficult. 'Leave it with me, we'll see what we can do, the price is good, so someone might be prepared to sell,' he tells his client. After ringing off, the salesman, a man in his early thirties, shirt-sleeved and displaying wide Wall Street braces, makes a few more keystrokes. In quick succession, two graphs appear on the screen – one of them portraying the movement of the share price of the brewery group over a five-year period; the other tracking it against the progress of the Financial Times-Stock Exchange One Hundred Share Index, popularly known as the Footsie. The graph shows that although the shares have been rising they have been outperformed by the index.

The salesman smiles, reflecting that one of the brewery's major shareholders may well be prepared to sell, given the higher price of the stock, and the prospect that by reinvesting elsewhere there will be a more profitable return. He keys in a few more strokes, and a printer at the end of the desk produces a sheet of paper with a breakdown of the company's major shareholders, in order of size of holding. Most of the names on the list are investment institutions, life assurance companies competing with the salesman's client, pension funds, and unit trust companies. But there are also some international companies and a handful of names of wealthy individuals. The salesman calls over a junior colleague, and tells him: 'See if you can do anything with this. We need a million.'

The young man returns to his desk, picks up his telephone, and starts making calls. Within 40 minutes he is back. 'I've got them,' he says, glowing with pleasure at his swift if unexpected achievement. The salesman whoops with joy, hits his client's number on the phone pad, and passes on the good news. He then walks over to market makers sitting at another, larger bank of computers, and asks them to execute the deal. As mentioned earlier, market makers set the price for shares and, within limits, are obligated to buy and sell at the prices they set. One of them keys in both the purchase and the sale: and the deal is complete. The salesman is well pleased. His firm's commission on the transaction will be about £150,000. A small percentage of that goes towards his annual bonus.

The stock market is not unlike that for airline tickets. You can pay £1,200 for a fully flexible economy return ticket to New York, and find yourself sitting next to someone who has paid £225 for the same class of seat, the identical meals service, and the same quarter bottle of Californian Chardonnay. The situation is similar in buying and selling shares. Various investors buy the same share at prices which show widespread differences, depending on the day or minute purchased, the volume bought, and the system used to buy them.

In share transactions in Britain a class system exists, just as such a system is pervasive in British life. However unlike the general class system, it is not based on royalty, privilege of birth or inherited wealth, but on real money and corporate power. As you might expect those with the most financial clout get the best deals and the hottest information. That this should be the case is of increasing concern to a number of consumer pressure groups and those few members of parliament who have had the wit to notice.

How it works in Britain is a depressingly familiar story. Those dealing in large blocks of shares in the companies that make up the FTSE 100 may post the price at which they are prepared to buy or sell their stock on the London Stock Exchange's electronic trading system. By doing this they can directly influence the market. If they effect a trade at the posted price they not only save on brokers' commissions but also on the profit the market maker takes by the spread between the price he buys at and that at which he sells.

The rest of us have to buy and sell our shares through the market-making system, which means that we buy or sell at a price set by a man – it usually is a man – in a busy dealing room. Since we cannot deal with market makers direct, we also have to pay a broker's commission as well as a dealer's spread. Those without a stockbroker pay even more, directly or indirectly. This group includes the majority of those who have acquired popular shares through privatization or the floating off of mutual assurance companies over the last few years. Abandoned largely to their own devices, they have sold out their share holdings through high street banks and building societies, many of whose front counter staff not only are totally ignorant of the working of the stock markets, but compound their ignorance by attempting to persuade investors to buy unit trusts and other packaged investment products of doubtful quality. They would be better off logging on to the Motley Fool on the Internet. The Motley Fool web site is discussed in Chapter 10.

Another pernicious aspect of the stock market's class system is the way in which it extends to the provision of information. Anyone can buy the *Financial Times*, of course, and it can and should be mined for information. But real-time share prices, and other up-to-the second market information, is only available to a privileged few who will wish to purchase it, which usually means the professionals. Computer services with real time prices and up-to-date news cost in the region of £10,000. At the next level down are Internet services and television programmes such as those provided by Bloomberg, CNN and CNBC. These are free, as are services like the BBC's Ceefax teletext, where the share prices are not current but are updated several times a day.

If you watch the football scores during a match's progress on Ceefax or Oracle, the ITV equivalent, goals are marked up almost immediately. It is strange indeed that a goal in a game of football is considered more significant than a share price movement that may affect many thousands of investors. Put the other way round, would viewers be prepared to accept a ruling by the Football Association that publication of scores could be delayed for 15 minutes because the rights had been sold to a media mogul like Rupert Murdoch? It is unthinkable. Yet the world's most important stock exchanges, including those in New York and London, have for years been able to get away with an insistence that publication of prices should be delayed 15 minutes except for those information providers that pay the exchanges a hefty fee. It is surprising that, in Europe at least, this practice has not been the subject of scrutiny by the European Competitions Commissioner, who would surely declare it anti-competitive.

In order to understand the class system of share dealing, it is worth examining in some detail the way it applies in the London market. This will also help small investors to comprehend why it is that it is very hard for them to compete in the day-to-day market-place, and why it is usually better for a private individual to stand back from the flurry of the trading floor and make medium-term, rather than short-term, judgements.

The principal shares traded in London are those in the companies that make up the FTSE 100 index. Since mid-October 1997 these shares have been traded on the Stock Exchange's order book system – known as SETS, an acronym for Stock Exchange Electronic Trading System. This matches orders placed electronically by prospective buyers and sellers, partly replacing the quote-driven system where deals were done by telephone.

So instead of agreeing to trade at a price set by a market maker, as described later, buyers and sellers of large blocks of stocks can advertise through their broker the price at which they would like to deal, and then choose to wait for the market to move in their favour, or to execute the deal immediately at the best price currently available. Only members of the London Stock Exchange can enter orders directly into SETS.

Under the system, investors wishing to deal will contact their broker by phone or by electronic mail, and agree the price at which they are willing to buy or sell a particular stock. The broker will enter the order directly into the order book, and it will be displayed anonymously to the entire market.

For example, the broker could open his screen on the stock and find an investor wants to sell 4,000 shares at once, at the 'best price' available. At the time the best 'buy' order available is for 17,800 shares at 938 pence. The 'sell' order for 4,000 shares will automatically trade against the 'buy' order – leaving 13,800 shares at 938 pence still on the order book. The second the order is executed, the trade is automatically reported to the Exchange, and the market informed immediately.

This is only one type of share trade using the order book system. Another common deal is the limit order. Here the investor posts specific details of the proposed trade – the number of shares, the price and the date upon which the offer will close. These limit orders sit on the SETS electronic order book until either they are matched or they pass the expiry date. Another is the execute and eliminate order. It sounds like a command from the old Soviet KGB, but in fact is very similar to an 'at best' order, but with a limit price specified.

Automatic execution through the order book takes place between 08.30 and 16.30. From 08.00 there is a half-hour period during which orders can be added or deleted in readiness for the trading day. In the half-hour between the end of the trading day and 17.00 there is a housekeeping period during which orders that have not been executed may be deleted if brokers do not wish to leave them on the book overnight.

The introduction of this form of trading has made London more efficient, and brought it in line with its major competitors, who were threatening to take a great deal of institutional business because of the lower spreads and cheaper commissions available through order book trading. Until its introduction spreads in the old system gave market makers a turn of on average, 0.6 per cent, the highest of any big market. France, Germany, Italy and Spain were operating on spreads of one-sixth of this amount. It also created a big reduction in commissions.

Country	Size £bn	Type of Market
US-New York	4,300	Floor auction with electronic order routing
US-Nasdaq	870	Electronic quote driven plus limit orders
Japan	1,940	Floor auction and electronic order book
Britain	1,150	Mixed electronic order book and quote driven system
Germany	480	Mixed floor auction and electronic order book
France	340	Electronic order book
Netherlands	325	Mixed floor quote driven and electronic order book
Canada	300	Electronic order book
Hong Kong	300	Partially electronic order book (input on floor)
Australia	180	Electronic order book
Italy	165	Electronic order book
Spain	130	Electronic order book

Source: Credit Lyonnais Laing

So, as the table illustrates, in London and the other large financial centres, shares are no longer traded on a floor. Gone are the days when visitors could climb two storeys at the London Stock Exchange to a public gallery and enjoy the spectacle of scores of dealers clutching paper orders and milling round the jobbers as they set the prices. On busy days there would be a crush, and a great roar would go up when an item of news was flashed across the ticker screen. The old floor looked not unlike a flea market; the analogy is a good one for real bargains were struck every minute of the trading day.

The excitement has now been transferred to the dealing rooms of the large securities houses where, despite the arrival of order-based trading, the focus is still on the market makers. Market makers set the prices for all transactions other than those booked through SETS. Although, at the time of writing, the London Stock Exchange hoped that more than half of the FTSE 100 trades would be conducted through SETS by the millennium, the market makers and their spreads are still very much in evidence.

The job of a market maker is sedentary. They sit at their terminals all day, their only exercise swivelling in their chairs to shout across to a colleague or taking a 30-minute break to visit a gymnasium or squash club. Not all market makers can trade all shares; their bailiwick is those sectors in which their firm has elected and been authorized to make a market. Like the jobbers of the past, the market makers will typically specialize: for example, in oil stocks, the leisure sector, industrials, banks and so on. Once a bid and offer price have been entered, the market maker is obliged to trade at that price, although of course he can alter his figures at any time in response to market conditions – in other words after he has seen what the opposition is doing. The SEAQ system covers more than 3,500 securities, and is divided into three groups of stocks – alpha, beta and gamma.

As the name implies alpha stocks are the most actively traded shares, and market makers who buy or sell must immediately enter the trade into the SEAQ system. From SEAQ the trade details are passed instantly to the London Stock Exchange's electronic information service, which is available to traders, brokers and investors.

So, to take an example of an investor purchasing 500 shares in British Petroleum, how does the new system work? His broker or licensed financial intermediary will call up the BP page from the system, and see an array of offers from more than a dozen market makers, each of them identified by a code. One line will say 'ML 36–40 1 x 1'. This means that Merrill Lynch, for example, are prepared to buy BP at £10.36 and to sell at £10.40, and that their figure applies for purchases or sales of 1,000 shares or less. Another line might say 'DMG 36–41 1 x 2', indicating that Deutsche Morgan Grenfell will buy at the same price as Merrill Lynch, but that they will only sell BP at £10.41, and then only in units of up to 2,000.

Another page on SEAQ will reveal that ten minutes earlier there had been a large transaction of BP shares at £9.38. Assuming he wants to trade, the broker calls the dealing desk of his own or another firm and asks to buy BP at £10.40. If the broker's firm is also listed as a market maker in BP, the broker will try and keep the deal 'in-house' by persuading his own colleagues to match the Merrill offer, which they may or may not be willing to do. When the bargain is struck, the market maker enters it into the BP SEAQ page; other market makers, noting the transaction, readjust their offers accordingly.

Deals in beta stocks are concluded in exactly the same way, except that not all trades are logged, and there are fewer market makers, perhaps only two or three, who will usually be in firms that have decided to specialize in a particular sector, such as electronics or insurance. In the case of gamma stocks, only indicative quotes are provided, so that any broker anxious to consider a purchase has to call the market maker and negotiate a price, often based on volume. Many of the market makers in the gamma section may be regional brokers, who know companies in their area well and are better placed to hold the book than a large London conglomerate.

For the technically-minded, the SEAQ system operates on two dedicated mainframe computers, designed to respond to entries within one second, update information at a peak rate of 20 items per second, and handle up to 70,000 transactions an hour. In the event of a computer crash, a major fire or bomb outrage at the Stock Exchange, all the records would be saved, for parallel computers operate in another part of London and, for double protection, in the United States. The entire capitalist system is not likely to fail because of a power cut!

Brokers and dealers get their information through a personal computer, connected to the SEAQ system either by direct data line or, in the case of the smaller user or provincial broker, by a leased telephone line. Those who wish to use the system only occasionally may do so through an ordinary phone line, connecting their computer to the jack via a standard modem. Those on the move may use a laptop computer plugged into the telephone.

While equities represent the most interesting aspect of stock market activity, and offer the investor the greatest degree of risk and reward, it is important not to overlook gilts, as they are known in Britain, or bonds everywhere else. There is a substantial market in buying and selling these bonds, the prices of which vary according to how far out of line their fixed interest rates are with the standard rates of interest applying at the time in the economy. If interest rates are falling, then gilts with a higher rate will be sold at a premium to their basic price. As with equities, prices are set by market makers, drawn from 25 firms.

7   The Street

'I would rather be vaguely right than precisely wrong' – Warren Buffett.

'Risk arbitrage is not gambling in any sense. Traditional stock investing is much closer to gambling than is risk arbitrage' – Ivan Boesky, in his book *Merger Mania*.

'The New York Stock Exchange is perhaps the most substantial and perfect financial temple in the world' – John Rodemeyer.

Wall Street is the term used to describe the financial district of New York. Like the City, it occupies only a small area of the business capital of the United States. Wall Street is in lower Manhattan, facing out to the Statue of Liberty, and the stock market grew up there in support of the merchants and bankers who, two centuries ago, established themselves on the tip of the island, when it was the pre-eminent business centre of America.

In those days Wall Street was the most important thoroughfare. Cargo ships were moored on the nearby East River, and the commodities they brought were traded in offices and warehouses on what became known as 'The Street'. As in London, everything in the area was destroyed by a Great Fire: the one in Wall Street occurred in 1835, and the damage stretched from the present site of City Hall to the Statue of Liberty.

The New York Stock Exchange was founded on its present site, the block bounded by Wall, Broad and New Streets and Exchange Place, although it has been rebuilt several times since the construction in 1864 of Renwick's $2 million marble-fronted wooden building, highlighted by eight lacquered columns and a rococo cornice. The first New York Stock

Exchange was more like a gentlemen's club than a business centre. There were 1,100 members, and its books and records were as closely guarded as those of a Masonic lodge. There was an honorary president, with few duties, and two salaried vice-presidents, but they had little to do except open and close trading at the morning and afternoon sessions.

The Exchange conducted its business by way of auctions, not dissimilar to those used by Sotheby's in the fine art market. Sellers would hand in their shares to the vice-president, who would guard them rather like a cloakroom attendant at a large hotel. They would be auctioned in blocks, and sold to the highest bidder. Inevitably, as with real-estate auctions, some deals took place outside the room, usually in the street, and a number of sub-exchanges grew up, often handling specialist shares.

One of these grew into an exchange of its own, operating from another building in Lower Broad Street, where it was known as the Open Board, so called because access was available to anyone prepared to pay a $50 membership fee. Once inside there was no auction, no organization and no records were kept: buyers simply met potential sellers and dealt. The Open Board operated six days a week, and kept open as long as there were sufficient people about.

Out of this chaos developed the ticker, telegraph machines which simply listed the latest prices at which stocks were traded. As access to the ticker spread beyond Wall Street and New York itself to other American cities, further share trading exchanges grew up, using the ticker as a guide to prices.

This development was viewed with some alarm by the elders of the New York Stock Exchange. Although the ticker services generated more business, their activities were outside NYSE control, their prices were sometimes wrong, and they led to the proliferation of rival trading locations. So in 1885 reporters of ticker companies were barred from the floor of the exchange, and forced to purchase the information. Within five years the New York Stock Exchange had control of the ticker, and was able to insist that Western Union, telegraph company which distributed it, make it available only to licensed brokerages and other approved buyers. (This, as we shall see later, created an unfortunate precedent.)

By this time business had grown to such a level that the auction system could not cope. What took its place was a sub-system of specialist auctions within the trading floor. Legend has it that a broker called Boyd broke his leg and, finding hobbling around the floor on crutches difficult, remained at one post to trade his shares. After his leg had mended, he discovered that this mode of operation had become so profitable that he stuck with it, thus creating the specialist market-making auction system that still exists today.

I can find no evidence that this story is anything but apocryphal, but something like this happened, and provided the basis for present-day trading in New York. The NYSE believes it is the 'world's fairest, most open, and most technologically advanced marketplace'. These days about one quarter of the membership of the New York Stock Exchange are specialist market makers, operating in 66 units. These units operate as principals in the shares in which they specialize.

These specialists form about a quarter of the professionals working on the floor of the exchange. The others are the people they deal with – the brokers and traders. A broker buying or selling shares on behalf of a client in any of the over 2,000 issues listed on the New York Stock Exchange will go to one of the 22 trading posts. There he will approach market makers, rather as in London, in the old days, brokers used to seek out jobbers, and seek a price. The market maker is obliged to be ready to buy and sell, and he has to balance his own books. If he is left with an oversupply or shortage of stock at the end of the day he has to hold it in his own account.

In theory the market maker only changes his prices by notches: thus he is not supposed to react to any dramatic turn of events by radical shifts. In practice he is human, and will not want to pay over the odds for a share which is tumbling. Running for cover is not encouraged. On the other hand when large institutions trade very large blocks of shares, it is unreasonable to expect an individual to hold out against a hurricane. The New York Stock Exchange attempts to keep market makers on track by policing price movements very carefully, and by encouraging competition.

This competition exists, of course, within the exchange, but also from rivals. One of these rivals is known as the over-the-counter market, so called because share brokers anywhere in the United States or elsewhere can buy or sell stock for customers who drop by. This market is run by NASDAQ, an acronym for National Association of Securities Dealers Automated Quotation System.

NASDAQ

In the spring of 1999 an event took place in New York which those who remember the era of Chairman Mao Tse-tung in China would have thought inconceivable. The Chinese premier, Zhu Rongji, paid a visit to the market room of NASDAQ. NASDAQ is the fastest growing stock market in the world, and is America's second stock market, listing over 5,500 American and international companies.

The tour over, he presented Frank Zarb, chairman of the National Association of Securities Dealers with a red bull, exclaiming 'always a red bull', symbolizing the hope that the buoyant United States market would continue on a role for ever. Zarb replied with the announcement that he intended to open an office in Shanghai, China's business capital, as the 'beginning of a process to create for China a way to bring investors capital to growing companies'.

In the United States NASDAQ has done just that, raising money for some of the nation's hottest stocks – Microsoft, Intel, Cisco, MCI WorldCom, Dell, Sun Microsystems, Oracle and Yahoo. NASDAQ now has a market capitalization of just under $2,500 billion, and all trades are transacted electronically. Like Britain's SEAQ for which it provided a model, NASDAQ uses computers and telecommunications – the information-age technologies – to bring securities firms together electronically, enabling them to compete with each other over the computer rather than on a trading floor in a single location. All the information needed for trading is in the open, on the NASDAQ computer screen, available at the press of the button.

This, to my mind, makes it more effective. Most of the world's leading information technology companies agree, for they have chosen to list on NASDAQ. The fundamental difference is that a traditional floor-based exchange centralizes people in a single location where trading takes place face-to-face. NASDAQ centralizes the information, but then makes it available to those who need it wherever they are.

The central computer system for NASDAQ is in Trumbull, Connecticut, but there is a full back-up facility in Rockville, near Washington, in case of failure. Trumbull and Rockville are connected by 80,000 miles of leased telephone lines to 3,400 securities houses that use them to display prices at which they are willing to trade – as well as to report sales and purchases, and other market data. The NASDAQ system is always being refined and updated and is considerably superior to SEAQ. There is plenty of competition; for a typical NASDAQ stock has 11 market makers hungry for business.

NASDAQ market makers, which include large national full-service firms, regional firms, local firms, and wholesale market makers – are based in 38 states and in the city of Washington in which the organization has its headquarters. Securities dealers in over 6,000 offices have at their finger tips an exact, national, instantaneous wholesale price system, available in San Francisco, Chicago or Dallas at the same time as Wall Street. Indeed, it goes beyond that. There are over 8,500 quotation terminals outside the United States, most of them, about 5,000, in Europe, and NASDAQ plans to extend this.

The NASDAQ system is also of benefit also to others in the investment business, from brokers in San Antonio to the man on the stockbroker counter at the local shopping mall, and to those in London who want instant information about the American market. There is nothing to stop individual investors subscribing, and NASDAQ already has over 100,000 hooked up, including brokers who are members of the London Stock Exchange. Those who pay a small subscription have access to the system through a dumb terminal and a black and white monitor. By using a word code on the terminal keyboard, they can obtain on the screen a representative 'bid' and a representative 'ask' price on the stock; for example, if dealers or market makers have quoted bids on a particular stock of 40, 40.25, 40.5, 40.75, and 41, the representative bid would be 40.5. If those with a terminal wish to buy or sell – or if their customer so wishes – all they have to do is to phone their broker and seek a real quote, asking that it should be close to the representative figure on the screen, and stipulating, if they wish, how far from the figure they are prepared to trade.

Today in the United States there are at least four million online accounts and the trades represent 30 per cent of the volume on NASDAQ and the New York Stock Exchange. In 2003 the number of accounts could grow to 20 million or more with the value of the accounts reaching $3 billion.*

What is interesting here is that these are only online trades conducted through a discount broker like Charles Schwab. In future there is no logical reason why trades should not be made electronically directly between parties ignoring the stock exchanges altogether. As Peter Clay, a consultant at PA Consulting Group, put it: 'The one thing the financial services industry fears more than a bear market is disintermediation'. But there is no reason why electronic communications networks (ECN's) can't be established to provide an alternative to the more established markets so long as trades are matched.

NASDAQ has a more sophisticated, and more expensive, service for professional traders. In this case, having obtained a representative quote, a user may then seek actual quotes from the firms making the market in the stock. This is what would happen if an individual using the basic service were to phone in. The screen would display all those offering a quote, together with their names and telephone numbers, ranked in order of best price. The final barter then takes place over the telephone, and the new quote is input on the screen, with the computer updating the representative or average price.

All deals in securities that are traded regularly and in large volume – a list of about 3,000 stocks – must be reported within 90 seconds of the trade taking place. There are safeguards built into the NASDAQ system to attempt to prevent malpractice, and to seek to provide the investor with the same security that he had under the London jobbing system.

---

*Financial Times Review of Technology 6 October 1999.

Once registered in a stock, a NASDAQ dealer must be prepared to buy or sell at any time, in much the same way as a jobber was obliged to stand behind his price. There must be at least two market makers for each stock quoted.

A market maker whose spread – the difference between his 'buy' and 'sell' quotation – is more than double that of the representative or average spread, will be warned by the computer that his spread is excessive. The computer warning also finds its way into the directories of the National Association of Securities Dealers, which will almost certainly call for an explanation, and may take disciplinary action.

Another safety measure is a provision in the NASDAQ rules that when a member dealer buys on his own account and not on behalf of a client, he should do so at a price which is 'fair' in relation to the prices being made by the market makers. The factors which should be taken into account by both members and disciplinary committees in determining the fairness of such deals are set out in the Association's Rules of Fair Practice, and include the type of security and its availability in the market.

All members of NASD must be members of the Securities Investor Protection Corporation, established by Congress in 1970; this means that those who buy and sell through the system have exactly the same protection as they would if they were dealing on the New York Stock Exchange. If an investor, or anyone else, feels he has been maltreated, or that there has been malpractice, the SIPC will contact the Association, which maintains a three-year computer file record of every price movement in a stock, and may trace the history of the stock second by second, identifying when changes took place, who initiated them, and what was the root cause. With such a complete audit trail, investigations are relatively easy to conduct.

8   Europe Takes to Shares

When, in the winter of 1990, the Berlin Wall came crashing down, symbolizing the end of the Cold War, there was an atmosphere of unrestrained euphoria. Germany, at last, could be reunited. New democracies in Czechoslovakia, as she then was, Hungary and Poland would take their rightful place in the European Community. Ten years later they are still waiting.

The cost of rebuilding the East was put at about one trillion dollars – and there were only three ways in which it could be found. The first was by taxing those who might be expected to benefit from an expanded market – West Europeans. There were many who publicly favoured the creation of an aid scheme modelled on the Marshall Plan established by the Americans after the Second World War. Unfortunately no one was prepared to pay for it.

Some European industrialists, like Carl Hahn, then the chief executive of Volkswagen, made bold moves. VW acquired the Skoda plant in the Czech Republic and transformed it into a model factory. Percy Barnevik led the Swiss–Swedish ASEA Brown Boveri into bold new ventures. American manufacturers, like Coca-Cola, piled into Russia at huge cost. However most of Europe's large companies stood on the sidelines and watched. The banking sector looked for profitable ventures to support, but could only do so much. That left the stock exchanges, in Europe known as bourses, but many of them lacked leadership and cohesion.

With the exception of London, with its global rather than European vision, the bourses in Europe had historically been narrow institutions, living in the past, with little vision beyond the national boundaries of the countries in which they operated. Their early prosperity had, of course, been shattered by the Nazi domination of Europe in the Second World War, when the pool of capital in most countries was devalued or destroyed. But that does not wholly explain their relatively insignificant role in capital formation. The real reason is the dominance of banks, both as a vehicle for individual savings and a source of finance for industry. As Anthony Sampson explained in his book *The New Europeans:*

> The big continental banks evoke a much deeper dread than the British, partly because they have embraced industry with a closer hug. Their power goes back to the nineteenth century. The French Rothschilds helped to finance the railways in France and beyond, and their rivals the Pereires set a pattern for the 'universal bank', collecting savings from small savers and deploying the capital for the development and control of industry, which was followed elsewhere on the Continent. The French banks soon fell behind the German banks, who played a key part in the new industries, and used their deposits, and their customers' proxies, to establish controlling shares in the big companies. A German bank, as the saying went, accompanied an industrial enterprise from the cradle to the grave, from establishment to liquidation throughout all the vicissitudes of its existence.*

Even a writer with Sampson's eye for detail could find no room to mention the bourses in a comprehensive 450 pages. This is not surprising, given their low profile as pan-European institutions, and the lack of a truly European stock exchange. Still they are growing. In 1993 the combined market capitalization of all the European exchanges was little more than half that of London. By 1997 Germany's market had risen from one tenth of the value of London to a third. France's Bourse was a quarter the size of London. And, for the first time ever the total size of Europe's bourses exceeded London's market capitalization.

Today the European securities industry is on the move, fuelled by a wave of privatization as aggressive as that in Britain in the Thatcher years. The biggest of these, Deutsche Telekom, raised 20 billion DM in December 1996, with 690 million shares sold at 28.50 DM each. Deutsche Telecom is now an aggressive global company, competing fiercely and effectively with BT, the first of the great privatizations in Britain.

Also energizing the interest in Europe's stock markets has been a wave of mergers and acquisitions, a phenomenon little in evidence in the eighties and the early part of the nineties. The arrival of European Monetary Union and the introduction of a single currency has been the prime motivating force, but another equally powerful catalyst has been the trend towards globalization in business.

13 October 1997 was a particularly crazy day for the European markets, when news of six major cross-border mergers hit the screens involving capital in excess of $100 million. These were:

- a move by the Swiss Zurich Group to take over BAT's financial services company to create a new group worth $35.7 billion
- a merger between Britain's Guinness and Grand Met, with France's LVMH having a 10 per cent stake in the new $39 billion entity
- a merger between the Anglo-Dutch group Reed Elsevier and Holland's Wolters Kluwer to create the world's largest scientific and technical publisher worth $10.6 billion
- a hostile $7 billion bid by Italy's Generali insurance company for AGF of France
- a hostile $2.8 billion bid by Lafarge of France for Redland of Britain

European countries have now created hi-tech stock markets to match the new mood. The largest is the Deutsche Borse which replaced the federation of eight regional stock markets that used to comprise the German market. The regional pattern has, however, been retained as DB operates through a series of city exchanges of which the largest is the Frankfurt Wertpapierborse, or Frankfurt Stock Exchange, based in Germany's financial capital. It is the fourth largest exchange in the world, and can be accessed via the IBIS computer system or, electronically, on the floor.

The exchange is still controlled by the banks, who are very reluctant to loosen their grip on any aspect of the capital markets. It is run by a council of 24 members, elected for a three-year term. Besides bankers, council members include official exchange brokers, independent brokers, insurance companies and other issuers and investors.

The main German stock market index is the DAX, which is based on 30 most actively traded German blue-chip stocks. It represents over 60 per cent of the total equity capital of

German exchange-listed companies, and trading in these shares accounts for three-quarters of the market volume. Another index, the FAZ, operated by the leading German newspaper, *Frankfurter Algemeine Zeitung*, is also an important pointer, being more broadly based than the DAX.

For a time Germany was slow to embrace the tough regulations favoured in the Anglo-Saxon world, and discussed later. But these days tough rules are in place to fight corruption and encourage transparency. Based on the model of the US Securities and Investment Board, a Federal Securities Supervisory Office is tasked with uncovering and prosecuting insider traders and other miscreants as well as supervising disclosure requirements.

Transparency has become a much favoured word amongst stock market regulators, and is, of course, the opposite of insider trading. As in Britain, insider trading used to be the accepted way of doing things, but now companies who list on the German exchanges are expected to be 'transparent', which means they should let in as much light as possible on their businesses. This, naturally, is often the opposite of the inclinations of many senior executives and board members. To its credit, the Deutsche Borse worked hard in the latter part of the nineties to enhance transparency, even though, in the Borse's own magazine *Vision and Money*, the head of research at Commerzbank is quoted as saying that 'the majority of businesses still have some catching up to do'.

One interesting initiative, which would also work well in London, is the Germany Equity Forum. One of the services it provides is to give enterprises seeking capital a low-cost medium to profile themselves or to set out financing needs and offer investment opportunities. The Borse does not act as an adviser or mediator and does not take any responsibility for the accuracy of the information. What it has done is to run a Forum, the first of which was in Leipzig in September 1996. It now has an Internet site which enables companies and investors to publish bids and offers (htpp://www.exchange.de). This is a useful way of putting venture capitalists together with ventures, which, later in their development, may wish to obtain a listing on the Borse.

Deutsche Borse also provides an Internet share market database which provides online price and volume data for all shares, bonds, indices, derivatives, and foreign exchange instruments traded on German exchanges. This means that for the first time private investors will be able to access directly data that was previously available only to market professionals, including real-time prices.

Another initiative has been the Neuer Markt, which provides a framework for companies to meet disclosure requirements and gives investors direct access to company information. Members must agree to meet the most rigorous international standards of disclosure (as well as the German ones), must issue quarterly and annual reports in English as well as German, and provide regular events for analysts and investors. Despite these strong advances in recent years, there is still much work to be done, particularly amongst the medium-sized companies that care little about their global financial image, and often disregard the regulations.

Mainland Europe's second largest exchange, the Paris Bourse, has also radically transformed itself in recent years. Its fine historical building on Rue de la Bourse belies the fact that, operationally, France now has one of the most modern and efficient stock exchanges in the world, with both screen and floor trading, a modern transactions system known as Relit, and deregulated commissions for brokers. But it is still perceived to be over-regulated by the French government.

One interesting innovation from France has been the Nouveau Marché. This was specially constructed for small but fast-growing companies in 1996. By its first anniversary in March 1997, it had 23 listed companies with a total market capitalization of almost 9 billion French francs. In that time it raised 1.87 billion French francs of new capital.

The Nouveau Marché has many similarities with the US NASDAQ. It requires the publication of quarterly results. Investors are obliged to retain their shares in the company after quotation, and cannot just sell out to make a quick profit.

The six million Swiss are perhaps the most heavily banked people on earth, and once had seven stock exchanges. But the big three banks – Union de Banque Suisse, Swiss Banking Corporation and Credit Suisse – decided to put a stop to this, and withdrew their support from the four smallest. In the end Switzerland may well end up with only the Zürich Bourse, controlled by the banks. In Zürich there are no market makers and no brokers: virtually all the work is done by the bankers' representatives, who only abolished fixed commissions because the Swiss Cartel Office forced them to do so. Institutional investors are not particularly active: Swiss pension funds have only about 5 per cent in local equities, though this is expected to increase. Despite its strong role as a banking centre, Zürich is not an important bourse. The 12 major Swiss stocks are also traded in London, which handles a fifth of total Swiss trading volume.

9   Finding the Facts

'Ninety million households in the US manage their finances with a paper and pencil, compared with 10.7 million using Quicken. The competition is tough' –
Rod Cherkas, of financial software producer Quicken.

Within microseconds of a takeover bid being announced, a company's profits tumbling, a director leaving or the share price of a company moving up or down on any of the world's major markets, investors everywhere in the wired-up world will hear of it. Financial news travels faster than anything else.

Usually the professional investors hear first, and pay for the privilege. They also have the benefit of the instant interpretation of a highly specialized team of analysts and chartists. Until recently the ordinary investor was far behind the professional in the information chain, but the arrival of the world wide web on the Internet has made the situation more even. Let us first look at what is usually available to the dealer or fund manager in a large institution, and then compare this with the information that is freely available to all.

For the full-time dealer in a broking firm or institution there are online services which provide prices in real time. These, of course, are expensive, but for market makers competing with each other they are an essential tool of the trade. Other professional investors normally make do with less expensive electronic services, which none the less provide essential figures and information within five minutes of their release. The three leading players in this market are Reuters, the British news agency started in 1851 by Paul Julius Reuter using a flock of carrier pigeons, BridgeNews, and The Bloomberg, founded by Michael Bloomberg.

The basic Reuter source contains about 2,500 pages of information, which are regularly updated by some 400 contributors. Instruments covered include straight and convertible bonds, stock market indices, government and domestic bonds, warrants, swaps, euronotes and commercial paper. Reuter also maintains an accessible database, which covers almost 5,000 eurobond issues, in all major currencies. Another service, Reuter 3,000, provides a complete and continuous overview of market movements and relevant factors affecting currency futures and options, interest rate instruments and stock index futures and options. A real-time quotes service covers equities, options and futures, fed from stock exchanges around the world.

Some of the Reuter news services have become interactive – all or some of those who subscribe may use the terminals that are provided to trade on the information made available. Reuter currency services, for instance, link via satellite and high-speed cable foreign exchange dealers in more than 110 countries – and have become the world's de facto foreign exchange market. Money dealers may access real-time information on currency and deposit rates, employ a range of graphs and other analytical aids to help their decision-making, and then use the Reuter network to complete their transactions with counterparties. Regardless of location, a dealer can contact any other in the world in no more than four seconds. The average connection time is two to three seconds.

To contact a counterparty in Tokyo, a dealer in London or New York simply presses a four-letter code, or a single-key macro code stored in an address-abbreviation facility. This facility also stores frequently used phrases or sentences, and can instruct the system to find the first free counterparty on a list and send a prepared message. An automatic print-out records details of every transaction for both dealing parties. The network is secure and private.

Roughly a third of the world's foreign exchange is done through Reuter dealing screens, and another third is transacted by telephone after consulting a Reuter monitor. Clients, who include most of the world's banks, pay a rent for the screen and a fee.

Reuters continues to develop a number of other interactive services to meet the needs of international capital markets, and constitutes a major challenge to stock markets that do not move swiftly to offer electronic on-screen dealing. Already its wholly owned Instinet trading service in the United States is used by professional investors to trade most American equities. Instinet is legitimized because its subsidiaries hold membership of seven major United States securities exchanges, as well as in London.

Reuter is moving fast to take advantage of new technology. In 1992 it bought the television news company, Visnews, renaming it Reuters Television, and buying for it a significant stake in Independent Television News, which supplies news programmes to Britain's three commercial channels. It includes video clips in its main news services, and positions miniature cameras above the computer terminals used by specialist correspondents and leading market analysts so that it can include commentaries by them on major news developments.

The principal competition to Reuters comes from Bridge which is the largest provider of financial information and related services in North America, and the second largest, fastest growing financial news provider in the world. Bridge, which claims to offer financial professionals and individual investors the industry's most complete range of products, bought Telerate from Dow Jones, publishers of the *Wall Street Journal*, and is a formidable player in the provision of real-time news.

Bridge's information products include a wide range of workstations, web-based applications and digital datafeeds that provide comprehensive market data, in-depth news and powerful analytic tools. All products operate on a variety of computer platforms, including Microsoft Windows, Windows NT and UNIX. Bridge also offers one of the industry's most respected trading room and data distribution software systems, providing seamless integration of data and applications across multi-platform systems.

Bridge's newsgathering arm, BridgeNews, is one of the world's largest financial news organizations. BridgeNews leverages a network of more than 600 journalists in 100 countries who break economic, government, financial and commodity news that affect major and emerging markets globally.

Headquartered in New York City, Bridge claims that every

day more than a quarter of a million investment professionals at more than 10,000 customer firms, including investment and commercial banks, money managers, investment advisors, broker/dealers, traders, exchanges, corporations and governmental agencies rely on it for information.

Then there is the Bloomberg, the name of the user-friendly dealing and information terminal provided by the iconoclastic Michael Bloomberg. The Bloomberg is the easiest of the terminals to use, and also allows you to do other things than just trade and wade through financial reports. You can check an airline flight, send flowers to your wife or girlfriend, and check out restaurants. The Bloomberg service seamlessly integrates data, news, analytics, and email into a single platform delivering information 24 hours a day. It is particularly good at analytics. You can assess risk with a range of analytic tools, download a portfolio, create custom reprints to see if your portfolio meets your investment objectives, and keep abreast of important news. Traders can process thousands of orders simultaneously through Bloomberg's electronic communications network, and find out immediately the major holders of the stocks they are following.

Bloomberg is aggressive and entrepreneurial in the marketplace, has recently added bureaus and staff worldwide, and has a dedicated staff inspired by Michael Bloomberg's upfront leadership. Bloomberg demands and gets energy from his staff, insists they work at least a 10-hour day, and rewards them accordingly.

Television: Open for business

Television has also become a significant source of information on financial and business news, particularly in the United States, where there is a full-time financial network, CNBC, owned by General Electric. From modest headquarters on two floors of an office block in New Jersey, it broadcasts over American cable networks to over 40 million television sets. During stock market trading hours, it positions a camera permanently on the ticker of the New York Stock Exchange, so investors at home or in their offices can get the latest pricing information in real time. Throughout the business day it runs a programme sequence called Money Wheel, where breaking stories are discussed and analysed by experts and, in some cases, the principals. Out of market hours it maintains a series of other financial and business programmes, some concerned with personal investment, some with management and some with boardroom styles and practices. CNBC launched a European network in 1996, and covers all the markets thoroughly. Competing with CNBC is Ted Turner's Cable News Network (CNN) which, although a general news channel, devotes a substantial proportion of its programming to business, and has brief hourly market updates. In 1996 it launched CNNFN (CNN Financial News) in direct competition with CNBC.

Bloomberg also runs a cable television channel, which is broadcast throughout the United States and in many other parts of the world. Although it is more of a 'talking-heads' channel than CNBC or CNN it follows the markets closely, and has a number of interesting interviews and discussion programmes.

Another new global business channel is being launched in the autumn of 1999 from Dubai in the United Arab Emirates. Dubai is a major entrepôt of trade and business linking East and West, with substantial cross-shipments of goods and services between Asia, Europe, Africa and the Middle East. The channel says it will have a market-driven commercial perspective, and is likely to provide an interesting alternative to the New York-based services. It is available on cable and satellite throughout the northern hemisphere and in Latin America.

Europe's traditional broadcasters have been slower to develop financial output, and much of it is not very good. Channel 4, the network set up to cater for minority interests, abandoned its *Business Daily* programme in 1992 even though it drew good audiences. Following the new franchise round, the ITV companies dropped *The City Programme*, which Thames had successfully launched several years earlier. Channel 5 also dropped its early morning business reports. The BBC has *Business Breakfast* early each weekday morning, but the emphasis tends to be on stories about industry and the economy, rather than on the markets. BBC Radio pays some attention to shares in its late-night Radio 5 programme, *Financial World Tonight*, but it does not have the following or the quality of the programme of the same name that was broadcast on Radio 4 in the sixties and seventies. BBC's *Moneybox* on Radio 4, however, provides a good personal finance programme.

Then there are a host of telephone services. These range from the relatively unsophisticated, which enable you to make a phone call and hear a recording of the latest major share prices, to several well-developed schemes where once you are connected to the database, you key in a code from your telephone handset and hear the latest price of the share or unit trust identified by the code. Subscribers are given a free directory listing the code, and can build up a phone service providing information on their own portfolio. These services are not cheap. Usually you pay for premium rate calls, and it is much better these days to use the Internet, as discussed later.

Taking the media as a whole, there has been an explosive growth in the financial information industry, which has increased the pool of knowledge about the financial markets and the companies traded there to the point where it is now well beyond the capability of one person to digest it all. Gone are the days when a stockbroker would sit in his first-class rail carriage from Sevenoaks to Charing Cross and comb through the pages of the *Financial Times*, working out his share tip of the day. Once at the office, he would telephone his friends and relations, and they would all be on to a good thing. A former City Editor of the *Daily Express* once told me that he had bought a house in the stockbroker belt and always travelled in a first-class compartment so as to be able to pick up juicy tips from those who were habitually on the same train. The journey home would usually be spent in the buffet-car where, over a beer or two or three, the successes of the day and the tips for tomorrow would be discussed.

In the late 1950s, the City Editor was a man of great authority, with an arrogance that could come only from having a considerable following of small investors. I remember Patrick Sergeant of the *Daily Mail* informing readers, just before leaving for his annual holiday one August, that they should not buy or sell any shares until after he got back. Patrick was not amused when he returned to find an anonymous telegram saying: 'Now that you are back, can we buy? – signed Pru and Pearl.'

City Editors also conducted their business with a certain panache. They would arrive in the office after a long lunch, smelling of port and accompanied by a cloud of cigar smoke. Even today, several Fleet Street City Editors are provided with dining rooms, at which they entertain bankers and brokers and government economic ministers. One or two others have a regular table provided for them at the Savoy Grill.

These days most broadsheet newspapers have an army of financial journalists reporting on the markets. Then there are specialist publications, which include the *Financial Times*, *Wall Street Journal*, the *Economist*, *Bloomberg* magazine, *Fortune*, *Forbes* and *Investors Chronicle*.

In the printed word the *Financial Times* is the best guide for the share investor in Europe, while the *Wall Street Journal* leads in the United States. Those serious about the markets should take both, or read them on the Internet. There is also strong coverage of the markets in The Times, the *Guardian*, the *Independent*, the *Daily Telegraph* and *Sunday Business*, and in two American publications, the *New York Times* and the *International Herald Tribune*.

10 The Internet

The Internet is by far the best source of information for investors. It is available, on call, 24 hours a day seven days a week. Its information is usually up to date, and it is usually possible to find real-time share prices if you want to chance your luck as a day-trader, though I do not recommend doing so. It is much better to take common-sense judgements on the short- and medium-term opportunities that are available.

You can use the Internet in three ways. First to obtain hard facts and numbers. Secondly to carry out more detailed research into companies or countries in which you may consider investing. And thirdly to trade shares on line.

For the latest financial and business news it is hard to beat the web services of the major agencies, though the European investors may well find that afxpress.com will provide all their requirements. Bloomberg.com is also very good, and it is surprising how much expensively gathered information Michael Bloomberg is prepared to give away on his web site, which is a first-class product. Bridge.com is also another very good financial news provider, and I find these three sites more user-friendly and up to date than Reuters, which appears to use its site as a marketing tool. The result is that it is a rather bad one; I'd be much more likely to subscribe to Bridge or Bloomberg, having experienced their web sites, than Reuters. Of course most web sites are transient, and are constantly being improved and upgraded, so any comments must be treated with caution.

Generally the major financial newspaper sites are a bit of a letdown. At the time of writing the *Financial Times*' ft.com was undergoing major redesign, and the user may get the impression that its editors regard their paper product as omnipotent, because little attention has been given to meeting the everyday demands of the serious investor. Generally you have to wait for the paper product to get the analysis and comment that should accompany breaking stories. That said, its branch site FT-Quicken is good, allowing you to maintain a detailed share portfolio, and update it regularly on line. Dow Jones' wsj.com is better, but you have to subscribe to it, although it is worth the modest amount that is charged. For American business two really useful sites are nyt.com from the *New York Times* and cnnfn.com, which is very easy to use and claims seven million hits a day.

Many investors will want more than just information. This is where sites that offer tools to track and analyse your portfolio have real benefit. Unfortunately most of the best sites are only serving the United States as their major market, although the Fairfax Group's tradingroom.com.au is a good source for Australian investors. Two of the best United States sites are wallstreetcity.com and thestreet.com, and both have plans to expand in Britain. Another interesting American site serving global investment is worldlyinvestor.com, which has good coverage of emerging markets.

Some of the leading brokers offer all their research material online, which is a bonus for those who do not have the cash to become private clients of large securities houses. Probably the best is ml.com from Merrill Lynch, which is in the process of creating a global investor network.

Public institutions also offer huge access to economic and financial information. The World Bank, worldbank.org, the OECD, the World Trade Organisation, the European Commission, and many more. The best practice is to spend an hour or two searching for those that suit your requirements, using a popular search engine like Yahoo.

The browser should also not miss the Motley Fool site on Motleyfool.com. This was one of the first and most original web sites in the financial area, and contains a mixture of amusing and sound advice. When in 1993 the big information providers and stockbrokers were trying to come to terms with the Web, three young people, David Gardner, Tom Gardner and Erik Rydholm conceived a site that would actually help investors with a mixture of statistics and wry common sense comments.

This extract gives a good sense of what the Motley Fool is about:

Conventional wisdom: 'You should just let "experts" invest

your money for you by putting your money in mutual funds.'

Foolish response: 'Hmmm. Well, if you really have NO time or interest in managing your own money, this may be true. But did you know that more than 75 per cent of all mutual funds underperform the stock market's average every year? In other words, most of the Wise "professionals" out there are losing to market average year in and year out. They'll try to convince you to invest in their funds, of course, by using jargon designed to confuse or intimidate you, and by putting up colourful graphs of their performance. Unfortunately, this hoopla dissolves away very quickly underneath the Foolish lens which compares the actual performances to the market averages.'

Why is such a sensible site called Motley Fool? The name comes from Shakespeare's *As You Like It*, in which Jacques says 'A fool, a fool, I see a fool in the forest, a motley fool', going on to say he was 'ambitious for a motley coat'. Motley was the multi-coloured garment worn by Elizabethan court jesters, while Fools were paid to entertain royalty, and were the only people who could poke fun at the monarch without having their heads chopped off.

For readers who have endured an overdose of bank managers, financial advisers, insurance salesmen, accountants and all the other hustlers in the financial services industry an afternoon spent online with the Motley Fool is worth the time.

11   The Analysts

What if you don't have access to the Internet, or don't like using computers? To many of us it has become second nature, but I have friends who refuse to install email, are frightened of even the simplest of technologies, and cannot cope with a keyboard, let alone a mouse. To me this is akin to saying you cannot use a telephone, but you have to be tolerant. And fortunately for them they are still chopping down trees in Finland and Canada so that financial institutions can send out weighty newsletters by snail-mail.

These days almost all the major broking houses run their own publishing operations, providing material in print as well as on the web, though Internet users will, of course, be able to read it first. Still brokers pride themselves on being able to get their publication out fast. On Budget day, for instance, some broking firms, as well as a few firms of accountants, will have their analysis of the Chancellor's measures in the hands of important clients long before the newspapers arrive.

Brokers' publications fall into two categories. There are regular weeklies or monthlies which contain a detailed review of the major economies and their financial markets, and offer a number of recommendations. Their forecasts have a high reputation for accuracy, usually better than the Treasury's. Amongst the regulars are Morgan Stanley's and Merrill Lynch's monthly outlooks, which are always good reading. There are regular specialist publications also, such as Salomon Brothers' *Financial Futures*, and *Options Analysis*. Then there are sector or subject reports, which look at either a company or an industry in great detail, and come up with recommendations.

Investor Relations Managers

Companies themselves like to publish more information

about their operations, and the rise of the specialist broking press has been such that the financial directors of large companies, and their public relations men, often spend more time wooing brokers' analysts than talking to financial journalists. Many companies employ an investor relations manager, whose job it is to keep both institutional investors and analysts informed of the more favourable aspects of the company. They now have their own body, the Investor Relations Society. Many of its members have lavish expense accounts, and jet in and out of two or more European capitals a day, expending great energy and charm on their subjects. Things can, however, go wrong. I remember the investor relations executive at Olivetti wringing his hands at an unfavourable broker's circular on his company written by a very presentable woman analyst, and crooning down the phone: 'How can you do this kind of thing to me?'

In recent years increasing attention has been paid by the major European companies to soliciting investment in the United States, and those who have neglected this aspect of financial public relations have done so at their cost.

An example is provided by ICI, which maintains a full-time investor relations executive in New York to keep analysts at both institutions and broking firms up to date with the company's financial affairs. Some of the information is printed material, but another aspect of the job is to organize an annual road show to five American cities. There are also quarterly meetings allowing all major US analysts to meet the company's finance director and other top members of staff, and visits are arranged for those who wish to tour ICI's operations in Britain.

The Analysts

Once the analyst was the office introvert, who spent his day hidden from view in a corner behind a pile of dusty papers, fretting over obscure charts while his broking colleagues got on with the business of trading shares.

Securities analysts have now formed an industry in their own right, and have their own professional body. It is a highly competitive business, and one in which the rewards can be considerable. There are even annual contests for best analysts, and broking firms, sector by sector. The best known survey, now the annual Extel Ranking of UK Investment Analysts, was started in 1973 by Continental Illinois, and is based on a detailed questionnaire sent to investment managers of the major institutions. Only four out of ten bother to reply in detail, but this still makes almost 100, with over £600 billion of funds in their care, and the survey is self-perpetuating, as the winners can count on many a new job offer and a stream of telephone calls from journalists, merchant bankers, accountants and others also anxious to tap their expertise.

A similar analysts' Oscar awards takes place in New York, under the aegis of *Institutional Investor* magazine. Across the Atlantic it seems much more of a one-horse race. Merrill Lynch, the world's largest broking firm once nicknamed 'the thundering herd', has won the award for each of the past three years, and for 16 of the 26 years the contest has been going. The US survey is the result of 1,500 interviews with professional investors.

The top ten broking firms in London together employ over 650 analysts, of which about a third cover European and overseas sectors.

The Extel surveys also reveal how specialist analysts have become. The typical analyst covers three or four sectors of the market, and studies 38 companies. Their average age is thirty-three, and the typical member of the fraternity will have spent six and a quarter years in the business, and three and a half years with his or her firm. Fundamental research and field trips take up to two-thirds of their time – and they spend a surprising amount of time on marketing activities, frequently talking to the media. This partly explains why analysts, especially those who appear often on radio and television, are not universally admired, particularly by the chairmen of companies upon whose operations they comment.

The world of the analyst starts with the fundamentals – the numbers that are used to measure a company and to compare it with another. An analyst will work through these looking at the EPS, the PE ratio, the yield, the NAV, and the DE ratio. It is worth explaining each of these terms, because they have significance for the serious personal investor.

EPS, or earnings per share, measures the amount of profit after tax. It is sometimes confused with the dividend, but it is not the same. The dividend is the payout to shareholders which usually consists of only a portion of the profits, the rest having been ploughed back into the business. Some companies pay higher dividends than they should in order to retain the support of shareholders, and neglect re-financing their businesses. Earnings per share is a more accurate measure of a company's success, and a good EPS may be an indication of a company that is growing sharply. However be cautious, for there are many successful companies that are parsimonious with dividends, and which may well be of less interest to those seeking income rather than long-term growth. EPS figures can sometimes be deceiving when a company has sold assets during a trading year and added the amount that has been raised to profits. To avoid confusion the Institute of Investment Management and Research has devised a new standard for EPS which excludes both profit from asset sales and the tax thereon.

The PE ratio is one of the most widely quoted measurements. It gives you the earnings per share as it relates to the price of the share. A PE of 12 means that the share price is 12 times the earnings per share.

Yield is a key indicator for those whose priority is income from their investments. It expresses the actual dividend as a proportion of the share price. A yield of 4 means that the dividend provided 4 pence or cents for every pound or dollar of a share's listed price. As a share price rises, yields go down to the point where an investor will probably be deterred from buying the stock.

NAV is the net asset value, and is particularly useful as a measurement when takeovers are being considered. It is an estimate of what each share would be worth if the company were liquidated, all its assets sold, and all liabilities settled, leaving a residue to be distributed to shareholders.

Net debt or gearing measures the company's borrowings as a percentage of total assets, and comes into importance at times when interest rates are high. A highly geared company is often of concern to investors, because it has to trade profitably in order to meet interest bills.

The job of an analyst is part office-based, part on the road.

He or she – and there are an increasing number of women in the business – has access to high technology, particularly numerous computer programs designed to make the postulation of future trends easier. An analyst will also spend a lot of time on the telephone asking questions, as well as attending briefings and seminars. In recent years it has become customary for companies, particularly large companies, to make life as comfortable as possible for analysts, transporting them *en bloc* or individually to expensive country hotels, where it is possible for them to socialize with directors and senior management as well as to talk shop. A thorough briefing of analysts immediately after a company's results are published can be crucial in getting a good press, for increasingly newspapers are dependent on the views of analysts for comment. Expectations can be lowered, if profits are going to be bad, and vice versa. Some companies choose an exceptionally attractive venue for six-monthly or yearly meetings with analysts. Carlo de Benedetti, when chairman of Olivetti, favoured Florence, where the men and women from broking houses across Europe could sample art and Tuscan wine. British Airways sometimes flies opinion-makers in the City to a variety of exotic overseas locations in the old but not mistaken belief that the further away from home the closer the mind might be concentrated on the subject in hand.

Often it is the City public relations firm which oils the wheels of the information industry function.

Financial public relations companies like to think that they are a cut above their contemporaries in the West End who deal with products and services, and they probably are. Their senior people certainly exude more style, and maintain larger expense accounts. Their role is also much more important. There are legal obligations on companies who make financial changes to inform the press, and someone has to ensure that announcements are hand-delivered or sent electronically round the City at the right time, usually before market trading starts or in late afternoon. There can be no question of sending out details of an acquisition, or a rights issue, on an embargoed basis.

But City PR advisers are no mere messenger boys. In many cases they are the eyes and ears of a company chairman and, occasionally, his voice. Some company chairmen are gregarious and well-connected individuals, able both to project a positive image and to be sensitive to public opinions. The majority are not. A good PR person will be able to keep the chairman and directors informed of shareholders' opinion, what the newspapers are saying and, increasingly important, an assessment of political, Whitehall and Brussels opinion. If needed, he will be able to lobby politicians on the company's behalf. In major takeover activity, or in rights issues, the public relations man will also become a valuable aide to merchant bankers and stockbrokers.

The Chartists

Unlike the 'health warning' advertisements, chartists believe that past performance really is a guide to the future of share price movements, and go out of their way to prove that this is the case. Chartism goes in and out of fashion, and some of the best chartists – or technical analysts as they are sometimes called – command respect and a large audience whenever they make a presentation.

The chartist is particularly interested in market peaks and troughs, and believes that these high and low points can be predicted with a reasonable degree of certainty. Expressions like 'points of resistance' are important. Just as it is possible to foresee that house prices cannot rise beyond a certain point (because the ratio of borrowings to average incomes becomes too high) or that prices can fall no further (because demand will rise from those on lower earnings) so stock market chartists are convinced that it is possible to assess a share's intrinsic value.

By carefully plotting price movements over a period of time – an easy process with high-speed personal computers – a chartist can spot a trend, and recommend a time to buy or sell. That is the theory; in fact chartism is fallible. The chartists failed to predict the great stock market crash of 1987, but then so did most other so-called experts.

Those who wish to learn more about the charms of chartism would do well to go to their nearest business book shop, and browse through some of the many titles available. An easier option might be to use the *Financial Times* to plot the performance of the main indices, and to look at shares that, year after year, appear to better it. If you have a PC there are some interesting and inexpensive computer programs that enable you to do this.

Financial Advisers

With such a wealth of information available, to whom do today's investors turn for knowledge, and from whom can they obtain the most reliable advice? It is an obvious question, and it is perhaps the one that is most frequently asked by those with more than a few pounds to invest. It is also one of the hardest questions to answer.

One quite correct answer is no one. In the end the investor, whether the chief investment manager of a large insurance company or a widow in Worthing, has to make the decision as to which is the best vehicle for improving the value of his or her savings. It is possible, even for those who do not consider themselves financially literate, to have cheap access to a great deal of information, and even that is sometimes of less use than a hunch or an everyday observation. For instance, anyone who has watched the development of Britain's high streets over the past ten years will have noted the rise of Tesco. You may not make a quick profit on Tesco shares, but they will grow, along with British Telecom, British Airways, and smaller concerns like Forte.

But this is to avoid the real question. To whom can one turn? A bank manager, stockbroker, accountant, building society manager, perhaps. All have their place and purpose, but none of them is necessarily a good investment adviser. Today's bank managers prefer to lend money than to give investment advice, steering customers in the direction of in-house unit trusts, which have not been the best performers. Accountants are useful tax advisers, and usually save you the cost of their fee, but when one seeks investment advice from them, they can start talking about complicated accountant-run pension schemes for the self-employed, and property trusts. Building society managers live or die by the balances on deposit in their branches, so it is not easy to accept their views as impartial. This leaves stockbrokers, who can be either good or bad advisers, but mostly are a mixture of both.

Regrettably very few large stockbrokers seem to want to service individual investors, and an increasing number of firms will not deal with them at all, unless the clients are very rich. This short-sighted approach is in contrast to the interest shown in small investors in the US, where share shops are common. But it is typical of the patronising attitude of many in the City towards the average member of the British public.

It may well be that Britain will follow the example of the United States. There, sharebrokers take their business to the public, and in almost every prosperous suburb there will be one or more open-plan broking offices, laid out rather like a large travel or estate agent, where members of the public may call, enjoy a cup of coffee, and discuss their investments with a consultant. There is plenty of literature available, including both brochures and financial magazines; Wall Street prices run continuously on television monitors, and there is a friendly and unpressurized atmosphere.

It is a pity that one of the few equivalent places in Britain's high streets appears to be the betting shop. The emergence of independent financial advisers should have led to the development of money shops, but not very many exist. For the most part the advisers stick to insurance broking, leaving share dealing to the banks and big securities houses.

12   Using the Stock Markets to Raise Money

Almost every entrepreneur has a dream that he will be able to build up his own business as a private company, and then, because of its success and opportunity for further growth, be able to sell it to the market. For many the happiest solution is to find large numbers of individuals prepared to buy a total stake of say, 47 per cent, so that the original founder and his family may retain control, while pocketing the cash generated by the sale. The lucky ones who do this become instant multi-millionaires, and are still able to hold on to the businesses they started and to run them in much the same way as before.

So how can an entrepreneur use the stock markets for his own benefit? The cardinal rule is that there should be some other reason for turning a private company into a listed one rather than just to obtain a personal fortune. It would not be easy to bring a company to the markets if that were seen by the markets as the prime purpose. The most obvious attraction of going public is that obtaining a listing on any major stock exchange improves the standing of the concern and its products. There are very few manufacturers of branded products or household names that are not public companies or corporations.

Apart from obtaining a better image, becoming listed on a stock exchange also makes it easier, in normal times, to raise finance for expansion and development. Both investors and lenders have a distinct preference for an enterprise that is not the plaything of an individual, or a group of individuals. Even though it is still possible for one man to hold the reins of a large public company, there are many more checks and balances than on private companies, where clever accountants can play interesting games with the balance sheet. The accounts, and other indicators of performance, of public companies are closely scrutinized by meticulous analysts, who are always prepared to publish adverse comment where they believe it to be deserved. Thus most public companies are assessed with one objective – are they good investments? By contrast, the potential of private companies is not easy to assess, even when they are open to scrutiny; private company accounts are freely available only at Companies' House, and then usually one year in arrears. This alone explains why both institutional and private investors are reluctant to commit large sums to unquoted companies. What happens when the leading figures in a private company die? Their heirs may be hopeless businessmen, or may be forced to sell up part of their holding at an inopportune time in order to pay capital transfer tax. Father may drop dead just as the next recession is approaching: subsequent family feuding and a forced sale could leave the outside investors with little to show for their years of support to the old concern.

Another strong advantage to an expanding business in being publicly listed on an exchange is that it helps in takeovers. Instead of paying cash for an acquisition, a company can often provide at least a part of the cost by offering a share swap, as in the summer of 1985 when Guinness offered shareholders in Bell, the whisky distiller, paper worth considerably more than the market price of their own scrip. When an efficient company is taking over a dull one, shareholders of the latter are often only too glad of the chance of just such an easy escape route.

A further advantage of obtaining a listing is that the company attracts unsolicited funds. If they think you are doing well, any number of investors will buy your shares. Regular mention in the financial pages is useful publicity and, in the case of well-run companies, makes for easier relations with customers and helps when attempting to attract executive staff.

Going Public

When a company decides it would like to go public, it normally approaches a firm of stockbrokers through its accountants or bankers. There is then usually a lunch or dinner, a getting-to-know-you session at which little more will be achieved than a general understanding of the nature of the business, and its goals and aspirations. The directors of the company considering a listing will also obtain some idea of how the operation, which is almost certainly a lengthy one, is to be planned.

Once contact has been established, and a decision made in principle, a partner in the firm of brokers will seek a total brief on the company – particularly its management structure, strengths and weaknesses, labour force, present shareholders, competitors, and, of course, a detailed study of full sets of accounts for the previous five years. Quite often this study will show that a listing quote is out of the question. In Britain investors and fund managers are spoilt for choice, and with governments the world over off-loading billions of pounds' worth of assets in state enterprises, any company that does not offer first-class prospects will not attract support. To go down the road towards a listing, and to issue a prospectus, and then have to withdraw it, would be a costly mistake.

Assuming, however, that the feasibility study shows a good prospect of success, the next stage for the stockbroker is to visit the company and its major plants or operations and to see it at work. This will usually be carried out by a senior member of the firm, under the supervision of a partner. The staff member will also try to visit competitors of the company, to seek another assessment, although the need for strict confidentiality makes this aspect of the study difficult. A firm of accountants, not the company's own auditors, will also be commissioned to carry out a thorough investigation.

All this will have to be done within three months, if a reasonable target for a listing is to be achieved. The next step is for the brokers to prepare a detailed proposal for the flotation, which will, in effect, form the blueprint for the day-by-day progress towards the listing. The broker will suggest a price band within which shares might be offered – the decision on a firm price will come much later. He will set out a list of financial requirements which will have to be met and propose underwriters who, at a substantial discount on price, will agree to purchase any shares if the float is undersubscribed. The company will usually be asked to pay off all major loans – for no investor is keen on picking up a load of debt – and to revalue all its properties. This stage completed, the next step is to decide how the capital of the company is to be made available to the public. In most cases, this will be through the issue of a prospectus, offering the shares at a price expected to be lower than the price at which the company will start its life on the exchanges. In the main European markets such a prospectus is published in full in the *Financial Times*, and, occasionally, other newspapers. The prospectus is, in fact, an offer for sale. It will detail the price at which shares will be available, and name any proposed restrictions on voting rights. The terms of sale will be set out, as well as the names and addresses of the auditors, stockbrokers, bankers, solicitors and directors. There will be a full description of its products or services.

Isotron, a company providing the only independent gamma radiation service in Britain, published just such a prospectus. It devoted thousands of words to an extremely detailed description of its technological processes, and its business prospects. A large part of the prospectus was devoted to the curricula vitae of the directors and senior employees, right down to site managers. There was a chapter on safety procedures, while over a page of closely spaced print was devoted to publication of the independent report by accountants KPMG Peat Marwick. The reader was spared no detail, and the prospectus constituted an extremely thorough insight into the company.

Once the prospectus has been written, usually by the merchant bankers advising the company in association with the stockbrokers, the approval of the local exchange where the shares are to be listed must be sought. This is much more than a formality, and it is quite normal for questions to be raised on matters of detail. For instance in London the most pressing concern of the LSE's quotations department is to see that the prospectus gives as full and accurate a picture as possible of the company and its prospects, and it is unlikely that a document will pass through unamended.

The terms of sale vary widely. Sometimes an underwriting firm of brokers will agree to buy all the share capital to be offered for sale on a given day, and then do their best to dispose of the shares to investors at a sufficiently higher price to offer them a profit. Sometimes the shares will be offered directly to the public by advertisement; where this happens the underwriters will only have to take on the shares left unsold, and if the issue is a success, may end up with no commitment and a useful underwriting fee.

Finding an underwriter is usually not a major problem, for all brokers have a list of those they can call upon, whether institutions, investment banks or other financial groups. Underwriters do count, however, on the integrity and accuracy of a broker's recommendation. No securities house can consider accepting the job of arranging a flotation unless it is convinced it is a sound investment.

An increasingly popular way of raising the cash is through public tender – used by bankers J. Henry Schroder Wagg and Co. in the Isotron case mentioned earlier. Here 3,290,088 ordinary 25 pence shares were offered at a minimum tender price of 120 pence a share, the principle being that those prepared to offer a higher rate would receive the biggest allocation. Having received all the applications, Schroder's were left with the task of setting a 'striking price', not exceeding the highest price at which sufficient applications were received to cover the total number of shares offered. A public tender was also used by Schroder's and UBS Phillips and Drew in bringing Andrew Lloyd Webber's Really Useful Group to a full London listing.

Obviously public tender is a system favoured by highly successful, confident and relatively well-known companies. It is not to be recommended if oversubscription is thought unlikely. Since the price has been fixed beforehand, it also avoids 'stagging' – a stag being the individual who buys new issues in the confident belief that oversubscription will lead to the price rising sharply on the day of listing.

Whether stagging occurs in the majority of cases when the tender system is not used depends, of course, very much upon the price at which the shares are fixed for sale. Pricing can be the key to the whole issue. If prices are pitched too low, there will be a huge oversubscription, involving vast amounts of extra paperwork, the return of cheques, and the difficult job of selecting the lucky applicants to receive shares. The stags will reap rich rewards. If, at the other extreme, the price is pitched too high, the issue will be a disaster, and months, even years, of work will be wasted. There have been examples of both; where there is oversubscription, those applicants who are left out, or awarded derisory holdings, feel aggrieved, even bitter.

Fixing the price is not easy, however, because most companies are the prisoners of current events. A series of air crashes could damage the price of the shares of a manufacturer of jet engines, for instance. Inevitably setting the price is left to the last possible moment, with brokers and bankers using their experience to judge market conditions as D-Day approaches. The 40 days and 40 nights before and after the day of flotation are the busiest, especially in the offices of those directly participating. It is not unusual for the major people involved to camp in their offices during much of this period, and certainly holidays are out of the question. While the final offer documents are away at the printers, they just hope that they have got it right.

Whether a company goes public through a full float or sale by tender, it is a costly business. The experts needed – lawyers, investment bankers, accountants, brokers and financial public relations men – do not come cheap, especially in the City of London. There are few ways of doing it cheaper, but one of them is to arrange what is called a placement. In this case, the stockbroking firm buys all the shares and sells them direct to its clients, avoiding the cost of dealing. This method is used in small new issues in London or where there is unlikely to be much public interest. But even here, the Stock Exchange regulations stipulate that at least 35 per cent of the company's issued capital must be in the placement, thereby preventing directors from using the system as a ploy to pick up some useful cash while still totally dominating the company. At least one-quarter of the shares must also be sold to the public on the stock markets, which helps when open dealings start. A placement is considerably cheaper because the costs of advertising, printing and professional services will be much less, and there is no need for underwriters.

There is also the alternative of arranging an introduction, but this way of obtaining a quotation in London is only available to those companies that already have a wide distribution of shareholders, and where there is no immediate intention of anyone selling out. No capital is offered prior to listing, and it is therefore not necessary for the company to go through the procedures described earlier, or to issue a prospectus, although it is required to take an advertisement to publicize the move. This method is most commonly used when a large foreign company decides to have its shares listed in London as well as on its home exchange.

Raising More Money

The stock markets were founded to raise money for industry and to provide finance for great national projects such as railways and canals. They raised money with great success until the Second World War, and in the early post-war years it was the place where companies went for extra funds if they wanted to expand. Borrowing from the banks was, in Britain at least, considered expedient only for short-term finance. Borrowing from overseas – through instruments such as eurobonds, and more recently euronotes – was not even in the minds of those few City types who supported Jean Monnet's vision of an integrated European Economic Community. Raising money was the job of the Stock Exchange. Why go further than Throgmorton Street?

Things began to go badly wrong with the capital-raising function of the Stock Exchange when successive governments in the middle years of this century decided that the best way of paying for expensive public programmes was to tax the rich, which, to them, included almost everyone who did not belong to a trade union and pick up his wages in a brown envelope once a week. Income from share ownership was 'unearned income', and somehow thought of as less decent than interest obtained from a building society. Making a capital gain by selling one's own shares at a profit in order to pay for old age, school fees, or even a trip to the Bahamas, was regarded as sinful, and therefore had to be discouraged through extra taxation. Company taxes were raised, making it harder for businesses to fund expansion. And, in order to justify an ill-judged attempt to curb a free market for wages, 'dividend restraint' was imposed. With little point in investing either for capital growth or for income, investors followed the example of the trade union movement, and went on strike. In other words, they ceased buying shares.

The political effect of the onslaught on the investor in the 1960s and 1970s was to bring to an almost complete halt a stock exchange system which allowed development capital to be raised, pluralistically, by a large number of individuals and institutions, and to replace it by a more costly system of finance through banks. It seems unlikely that the trend will ever be completely reversed, but in recent years there has been an encouraging revival of capital-raising on stock exchanges, to the benefit of both saver and entrepreneur.

Today business school studies by Nobel Prize winners Professor Franco Modigliani and Professor Merton Miller show that the costs of debt and equity financing are comparable. The cost of debt – of course – is easiest to measure: it is the interest paid by the company on its bank loan or bond. Assuming the company is a highly credible and successful one, known as a blue-chip, it will pay a premium of about two per cent over a bond issued by a credit-worthy country like Britain or Germany.

The cost of equity is the dividend yield, which should be cheaper, but often is not. Dividends often depend on taxation policy. Raising money through the share markets from rights issues also strengthens balance sheets and prevents the kind of over-borrowing that has forced many large companies into difficulty.

Sometimes companies will want to use both methods. For instance a British company may use a rights issue to fund a UK acquisition, but, if seeking to take over a European company, could use a foreign currency bond to match the currency of the target company's country.

What happens with a rights issue is that the holders of ordinary shares in a company are offered further shares at a discount, usually substantial enough to make it attractive. Under British rules, such new shares must be offered to existing stockholders in quantities proportionate to their holdings. This is known as a pre-emption right, which has been abandoned in the United States. A lively debate has been taking place in Britain over whether this rule is sensible. In many cases not all shareholders are willing, or even able, to take up the rights offer. So, under the present system, underwriters have to be found who will. As with new issues, pitching the price right is crucial. If a rights issue is undersubscribed there is a danger that the share price will fall, even if underwriters have been appointed, and this would defeat part of the objective of the exercise, which is to raise more capital.

The most important question for a company making a rights issue is to decide on the terms at which it will offer new shares. Normally this is done by offering the shareholders the right to buy a number of shares at a special price for each share they own. So, for example, in 1990 the British brewing group Bass sought to raise £558 million by giving its equity holders the right to buy one new share for every five they already owned. This is known as a one-for-five issue. In order to persuade shareholders to subscribe to a rights issue, the price has to be a worthwhile discount to the prevailing market price. But this does not mean that rights issues present shareholders with a bargain – an offer they cannot refuse. As soon as a rights issue has been completed, the price of the existing shares usually falls to reflect their dilution as a result of new stock on the register.

The small shareholder offered a rights issue is often in a Catch-22 situation. If he takes up the offer he has to dip into his savings and increase his risk exposure to the company concerned; in other words an additional investment is forced upon him. If he does not take up his rights he may sell them to a stockbroker for the difference between the rights price and the market price, but unless there is a substantial volume of shares involved the commission is likely to be prohibitive. If, as often is the case, you do nothing at all, the company will automatically sell your rights for you, and pay you the proceeds.

Rights offers are usually contained in a long and arcane document preceded with the suggestion that if you do not understand it you should see a stockbroker. Many people, particularly those who have not paid close attention to their investments or who have inherited equities, mistakenly throw these documents into the rubbish bin, and lose out.

After the deregulation of Britain's financial markets at the time of Big Bang in 1986, many people believed that companies would move across to the American system of placements, described earlier. They reckoned without the big pension funds and life assurance companies, which dominate the British markets and who were jealous of their automatic right to get a slice of anything new going. These institutional investors formed a cosy cartel, which called itself the 'Pre-emption Group', and set itself the goal to protect at all costs the right of existing shareholders to get first refusal of any new shares. At the time this group was established, the British government was supporting a change in the rules, which would have allowed companies to raise additional capital directly from new shareholders.

The Pre-emption Group frustrated this change by introducing a rule book binding on all its members. One of the guidelines was that in any issue of more than 5 per cent of a company's capital, the existing shareholders had to be given first call. Of course, as long as the institutions stuck to their own rules, their dominance in the market was such that nobody would be able to change matters. And, in Britain at least, so it has proved.

A rights issue is not cheap, which is one of the main arguments against this form of raising additional capital. First there are underwriting fees, paid by the company seeking to raise the money to the merchant bank or securities house managing the issue, and to those who have undertaken to buy any unwanted shares. These fees come to about 2 per cent of the amount of money raised. Then there is the paperwork – fees to lawyers, accountants and public relations consultants, plus the actual cost of printing and distributing the substantial amount of documentation necessary. Add to this the discount which must be offered to make the rights issue attractive – a figure of around 20 per cent is common practice – and it is easy to see why many a corporate financial director would rather go to see the company's bankers or, if it were possible, to arrange a placement.

An alternative to a rights issue is loan capital, which may be raised on the Stock Exchange either through unsecured loan stock or convertible stock. Loan stock is usually issued only by blue-chip companies. A company without a top rating would not find investors ready to buy it even at very high interest rates, and might offer the inducement of convertibility to enable the holder to convert all or some of the loan stock at a later stage to equities.

If a company is planning to modernize its plant to increase

output and productivity, loan capital can be a particularly attractive vehicle. The interest paid is deductible before corporation tax is payable, so the company's tax bill is reduced. And as output rises, and hopefully profits, so does the company's share price, making it beneficial for the shareholders to make the conversion.

As with new issues, there are several ways in which a stockbroker can obtain loan capital for his clients. He can arrange for a full prospectus detailing the offer to be prepared, published and advertised, and wait for the response, usually stipulating preferential treatment to existing shareholders. He may, if he chooses, place the loan stock with institutions direct – unlike placements with new issues, where a proportion has to be offered on the Stock Exchange. Or he may limit the offer to existing shareholders, an unlikely course because especially attractive terms are usually necessary to get full support. A placement is usually much more efficient.

Then there is the bond market, of which the eurobond market is the best known. Not long ago, only governments of stable and prosperous democracies and large international institutions such as the World Bank and the European Investment Bank would go to the bond market for funds, by issuing securities at good interest rates with maturity dates 10 to 20 years away. Mostly denominated in dollars, these securities offered large institutional investors an attractive hedge against the fall of sterling and against inflation. The introduction of the single European currency has brought a spate of euro-dominated corporate bonds to the market as companies begin to exploit a new capital raising opportunity.

Taking AIM

Money can, in theory, be raised for small and medium-sized go-ahead businesses through the junior stock exchange, better known as AIM, the successor to the Unlisted Securities Market. Similar markets have evolved in the United States and France, and the idea has widespread political support because small businesses are seen as major sources of job creation, technological innovation and entrepreneurship.

The high-interest-rate environment of the past few years has compounded the financing problems of the growing company, but AIM does offer those who have a case and can present it well the chance not only of raising capital for their expansion, but also of becoming rich in the process.

AIM offers all the benefits of the stock market, such as the opportunity for a higher public profile, and access to new capital and investors, with a much simpler entry structure than going for a full listing. For instance, there are no restrictions on the size of companies who join, the percentage of shares to be placed in public hands or how long they have been operating.

The key to AIM, and what distinguishes it from the Unlisted Securities Market, is the compulsory appointment to AIM-listed companies of two key people – the nominated adviser and the nominated broker, each drawn from specialist corporate finance companies which have been approved by the LSE.

The nominated adviser, who could be a stockbroker, accountant or banker drawn from a list of about 70 people, has the responsibility for deciding whether a company is suitable for the market, and for making sure it conforms to the AIM rules. Once listed the company must retain the adviser to keep it on track and to make sure it fulfils its obligations, which include disclosing all material information to investors. The nominated adviser has to undertake to be available at all times to advise and guide the company's directors on the AIM rules. The nominated broker has to be a member of the Exchange, and, in the absence of a market maker, provides a means for investors to buy and sell the company's shares.

AIM is clearly designed for professional, rather than amateur investors, and is for the risk-taker who accepts that not all young and growing companies succeed. It is of particular appeal to the large number of fund management groups that specialize in investing in smaller companies.

AIM companies do not have to be British, nor of a certain size, nor do they have to prove a lengthy trading history. But they must be public companies, registered under the laws of their country, and have published accounts which conform to proper internationally accepted accounting standards.

Before being admitted to AIM, the company has to publish a prospectus not very different from that required for a full listing; this is required whether or not the company intends to raise funds. The prospectus has to include a description of the securities to be traded, a full description of the company and its principal activities, the company's financial history and performance, details of the management, the directors and their personal business histories, and the names of substantial shareholders.

AIM shares are traded on what is called SEATS PLUS, which enables buyers and sellers to trade with each other through the LSE. They can do this either through a market maker, if there is enough of a market to justify one, or by an order board, which publicly displays orders to buy and sell shares, and allows trades to be executed automatically.

The service also allows financial information about each company to be entered by the nominated broker, thus helping investors to evaluate the shares. By the turn of the century the AIM exchange had raised well over £2 billion with its listed companies having a market capitalization of £6.5 billion. Of the 271 companies on AIM, all but 18 were British. Those listed included several football clubs – Birmingham City, Charlton and Chelsea Village to name but three – leisure companies, Internet firms, privatized railways recruitment consultants and wine importers.

A comparable operation exists across the Channel in France, where the Nouveau Marché was set up in 1996 to cater for small and fast-growing businesses. This also has relaxed joining rules so that, for example, new companies do not have to provide three-year financial projections, but must provide quarterly results. At the time of writing the number of companies listed on the Nouveau Marché was measured in tens rather than hundreds, but since its launch the index has grown by more than 50 per cent.

The problems of raising money for small companies in Britain are not confined to the equity sector; banks have also had difficulty in providing adequate funds at a reasonable price and on reasonable conditions. Despite attention-grabbing advertisements proclaiming their support for small business, the banks have failed to win many friends in this area. Under pressure to improve their margins and the quality of their loans following the mistakes of the 1980s, the high street banks have demanded interest rate margins and levels of security that make it very difficult for a small business to establish itself. HSBC as good as admitted this when its chief executive suggested that the best way for the small business sector to move forward would be if there were some kind of government support or guarantee for small business loans. He has a point, but the British government had its fingers badly burnt with the ill-fated Business Expansion Scheme which was largely used for property-backed ventures, many of which collapsed in the early 1990s.

Across the Atlantic, the NASDAQ market discussed earlier has provided the capital support for some of the most dynamic and innovative companies in the United States – Microsoft was founded in this way. Of the 100 best-performing companies, 75 have had their first public offerings in the past 15 years. NASDAQ listings contain hundreds of quality young companies whose securities trade in large volumes. NASDAQ has recognized that small companies are in the forefront of economic opportunity: small to medium-sized companies have created most new jobs in the United States in the past ten years.

The number of companies traded on NASDAQ expanded rapidly in the 1980s, from 2,894 in 1980 to 4,132 in 1990. This 43 per cent rise in the number of companies generated a rise in market capitalization of 155 per cent to $311 billion. Most of these have come to the exchange after an IPO (initial public offering).

A company seeking an IPO in America will normally be advised by its investment bankers to offer its stock at 10 to 15 per cent below trading expectation in order to attract suitable support. The bankers will produce a highly detailed prospectus, with considerable attention paid to competitive advantages compared with other listed companies operating in the same field. The Securities and Exchange Commission has a complex set of rules governing the issue of a prospectus, the foundation stone of which is full disclosure of anything likely to be relevant to an investor. But this rigorous attitude pays off; it gives the investor more confidence. In the United States a prospectus must include information about products and services, manufacturing facilities, competition, and possible risks – apart from full financials – and omission of information, or inclusion of misleading information, can provide a valid cause for a class action lawsuit. Once a prospectus has been filed with the SEC, the officials review it, and come back with comments, suggestions and criticisms.

Once a public offering has been made and the company is trading, it is subject to strict rules on corporate governance and the provision of information. There must be a minimum of two independent directors on its board. There is a total ban on the issuing of any preferential shares, or taking any action that would restrict or reduce the voting rights of ordinary shareholders. The company must also complete SEC documents 10-Q and 10-K which require disclosure of a wide range of information, including executive compensation, and securities ownership of certain beneficial owners and managers.

There is also the NASDAQ Small-Cap Market, which has about 1,200 smaller companies listed. The requirements for listing on this market are substantially less than those for NASDAQ itself, and it is used as a conduit to the main exchange.

13   Selling the Family Silver

'It's like selling the family silver' – former British Prime Minister Harold Macmillan, speaking in the House of Lords.

'I am not able to say myself whether it will be worth all the labour involved in privatization. I do not know. I think we shall find out only a lot later on' – Sir Denis Rooke, chairman of British Gas.

'Get it out . . . get it sold' – Kenneth Baker, when chairman of the Conservative Party.

'Privat: Middle English proverb from Latin, privatus, not belonging to the State, not in public life, deprived of office, from the past participle of private, to deprive, release' – American Heritage Dictionary.

Twelve Russians waited patiently in line for what, to them, was the sale of the century. This was not the type of queue so familiar in the 1960s and 1970s for bread, meat or items of everyday clothing. The Muscovites had come to buy shares in one of the country's best-loved concerns – the BBC, or Bolshevik Biscuit Corporation, which, in earlier times, had held 12 per cent of the Soviet market for cookies.

Each of them held a voucher worth 10,000 roubles, issued by the Russian government, entitling the holder to exchange it for shares of equivalent value in any enterprise offered for sale by the Ministry for Privatization. Advising the ministry were dark-suited experts from two Western financial institutions, Credit Suisse First Boston, and the European Bank for Reconstruction and Development. As they advanced to bid for their shares, the shabbily dressed men and women paid scant attention to the documentation set out on the tables before them. But their questions showed their relish for their proposed investment, as they asked: 'What will the return on capital be?', 'What are your profits?', 'What are your marketing plans?'

That day was the first time in Russian history that ordinary men and women had been able to bid for shares. Though the sale was not reported on television news bulletins in Europe or America, history was being made. Three years earlier, confounding Lenin's predictions, communism as practised in the Soviet Union and its Warsaw Pact allies had collapsed, leaving an economic shambles as serious as that faced in Germany at the end of the Second World War. New, democratically elected leaders sought to rekindle their economies by resorting to privatization: putting the ownership of enterprises into the hands of individuals and private institutions rather than under the control of the state.

Privatization has come a long way since it was pioneered in Britain by Margaret Thatcher's Conservative government on the idea of the management guru Peter Drucker – it is now a philosophy which has swept the world. One by one, governments have been divesting themselves of great state-owned corporations. Britain led the way in ridding the taxpayer of the burden – and the public servant of the responsibility – of huge utility businesses like power and gas supply, telecommunications and airlines. Five years after people queued in the streets of London to buy shares in British Telecom, the Poles and the Czechs were forming their own lines to buy assets once controlled by the communists. Now privatization has reached Africa, Asia and Latin America.

Alas, in Britain a brilliant idea has been poorly executed with the result that very few members of the public have ended up with more than a handful of shares. Instead of encouraging saving, privatization bred stagging – making a capital gain by selling equity at a profit immediately upon acquisition. The issues were priced too cheaply, and the City made huge profits, leaving a nasty taste in the mouths of ordinary families who came to believe that share-trading was not for them.

Yet it is unlikely that the burst of interest in share ownership, particularly among the working classes, would have come about if the British Telecom float had not taken place, with its hype, touring road shows, television campaign and gimmicks like bonus shares and vouchers to help pay the phone bills.

Even more hype went into the sale in December 1986 of over four billion shares in British Gas, with the introduction to the nation's television screens nightly of an ubiquitous but enigmatic character called Sid. Clever if unsubtle advertisements by the Young and Rubicam agency urged viewers to 'tell Sid' about the opportunities for the public to buy shares in British Gas. One even had a pigeon fancier releasing his bird and saying 'There y'are my darlin', just go and tell Sid'. Right to the end of the campaign, Sid was never to be spotted; in the very latest advertisement a near-demented potential shareholder was seen climbing a mountain peak and peering through the mist crying 'Sid' at a shape that turned out to be nothing more than a startled sheep.

The British public gratefully accepted the offer – and why not? As with British Telecom, the government had priced British Gas attractively and with a forthcoming election in mind – those who sold quickly were rewarded with a capital gain in excess of 20 per cent, and those who held the stock could look forward to cheaper fuel bills with the prospect of gas vouchers in addition to normal dividends. For every 100 shares bought, investors received a voucher worth £10 payable over a two-year period.

Once British Gas was safely out of the way, the government set about another major sale, that of British Airways. This was followed by British Steel, the nation's electricity industry, the water authorities, and the railway network. The *Economist* saw it as 'the largest transfer of property since the dissolution of the monasteries'.

From Warsaw to Washington workers now own shares, but there is a considerable debate on the effectiveness of employee ownership. So far there is little evidence to suggest that employees use their position as shareholders to influence boards, although in some cases workers have delegated their voting rights to trades unions. Even in companies where generous workers' participation exists, their collective holding seldom rises above 5 per cent. There is also an argument that workers should behave in exactly the same way as prudent investment managers, and spread a share portfolio over a number of stocks to minimize risk. Certainly an employee with shares in his employer's company should be wide awake to the downside possibilities – in other words that he may lose all or most of his investment.

Another complication comes when employee share ownership is mistakenly seen as a form of performance-related pay. Share ownership is not, and should not be seen as, an alternative to incentives. Share ownership gives employees a stake in the capital of a company, regardless of whether individually or collectively they have made a positive contribution. Profit-related pay and bonus schemes, which may be based on meeting budget or on the return of capital, however desirable, are quite separate.

Privatization: Privileges for the Workers

Few employees have fared so well as those working for privatized concerns in Britain, for in almost all cases they were offered privileged treatment both on price and allocations.

Let us look at just one example: the employees of Northumbrian Water, the most over-subscribed of the ten new water companies. Those who did not live in Northumbria were restricted to just 100 shares each, and even the customers were allocated only 200: hardly worth the bother, and almost a waste of time. Those who worked for the company, however, had every reason to smile, for they were entitled to apply for and get up to 5,000 shares. Workers at the other companies received the same preferential treatment.

The Northumbrian shares were priced at 240 pence, payable in instalments, but water employees were able to invest at a 10 per cent discount. When trading started on the share markets, the opening price showed a premium of 60 pence a share. A worker taking his full allocation would have shown a paper profit of about 84 pence per share.

The water workers – along with other employees of privatized concerns – have also enjoyed other special privileges denied to others, the most significant of which is exemption from the punitive taxation imposed on their counterparts who work for other companies seeking extra capital through rights issues. Although companies offering rights issues normally allocate employees' shares – through the distribution of the so-called pink forms signifying a priority offer – those workers who take advantage of this have to pay tax as PAYE on the premium to the issue price when the share starts trading, as if it was income. Indeed so unfair is this rule that most employees end up having this tax deducted from their wages before they are able to dispose of the shares. The workers of privatized companies face no such intolerable burden.

The 90,000 workers of British Gas were also given generous treatment, which cost the taxpayer a total of £54 million. Each employee was awarded £70 worth of shares, plus a further £2 worth for each year of service. Those able to invest their own money were given two free shares for each one bought, up to a limit of £300 worth of free shares. Those inclined to dig deeper into their savings could buy up to £2,000 worth at a 10 per cent discount. Pensioners were also each given about £75 worth of free shares. This was in sharp contrast to the parsimony of British Telecom, whose employee shareholders missed out.

In all the major privatizations so far, the majority of employees have taken up their entitlements, though many later sold or reduced their holdings. Foolishly perhaps, most employees sold their holdings on the market, rather than to work colleagues or trade unions, for had they adopted this latter course they could have wielded more influence in their companies. To some extent this happened in the case of British Airways where 5,000 employees gave their union a proxy vote over their shares.

The system used in Britain to enable workers and members of the public to buy shares was not suitable for former command economies like Russia and Eastern Europe, for two reasons. First, the public did not have the cash to buy privatization issues. Second, it proved difficult, sometimes impossible, to put a value on the former state enterprises being sold, especially as a large number of them were technically bankrupt. Many governments overcame the first hurdle by giving their citizens vouchers whose only value was as an instrument to be exchanged for shares. If, in so doing, the citizens found themselves in possession of shares that were worthless, at least they had not lost their own savings.

Sale by Mutual Consent

Just when the flow of British privatization bargains had dried up another trend emerged. It was called – in another massacre of the English language by public servants – demutualization. For years the building societies – one of Britain's most established institutions – had competed with each other in a mad scramble for a prime space in the high streets. They had been operating, literally, for the mutual benefit of their members.

Building societies were created to enable people to buy houses. At its simplest, the concept of the building society movement was that some members lent their savings to the societies at one rate of interest, and those buying borrowed money to purchase their homes at a higher rate. The money accumulated because of the difference between the two rates, both of which moved up and down more or less in line with market forces, went to pay for expenses, or to boost reserves. While the societies noisily defended the level of management costs and the need to establish visibility in the high street through branch networks, many felt there were inefficiencies in the system. (Actually the relative efficiency of many building societies pointed up the inefficiencies of the high street trading banks.)

This principle of mutuality also extended to a large number of life assurance companies. Their difference between income and expenditure also went towards building up lavish reserves, generous staff benefits for employees, especially senior management, and bonuses for policyholders possessing 'with-profits' endowment policies. Quite often building societies worked alongside the assurance mutuals, encouraging individuals to purchase homes on an interest-only basis with the capital repaid on the maturity of the endowment policy. This inefficient form of home purchase was for many years encouraged by the government, which made both the interest charges and endowment assurance premiums tax deductible, thus conferring a substantial benefit to the higher-paid at the expense of those who could not afford to buy property.

As successive governments stripped away most of these tax benefits both building societies and life assurance mutuals found they had to compete in the real world, and many of them did so very well. The Conservative government also introduced legislation to encourage competition in the financial sector, and many organizations from both groups felt they would be able to hold their own against public liability companies.

Many, but not all, also felt they would be best able to compete by being on level terms, and becoming a fully listed public liability company with the ability to raise funds on the stock market. One of these came from the East Anglian city of Norwich, where not only is it the biggest source of employment but in 1995 surprised the local community by offering a job to every school leaver in the county of Norfolk with A levels.

For all its humble origins the Norwich Union, at the time of its flotation, was a global business with branches worldwide. Its approach to 'demutualization' was even bolder, because not only did it offer its members, those holding 'with-profits' policies, a free windfall of shares worth between £800 and £4,000, depending on the size of policy, but it also raised about £1.8 billion of new money with an additional offer to policyholders. By the time it had joined the Stock Exchange and its shares were trading on 16 June 1997, it was one of Britain's top 50 companies, worth around £5.5 billion. At the time of writing the speculation is that it will be taken over by a high street bank.

Many of those receiving the windfall shares – for unlike privatization issues they did not have to pay anything for them – sold them shortly after 16 June, pocketing the cash in time for the family summer holiday. However those who did not sell received an added bonus: under a government dispensation they were able to transfer the shares into a personal equity plan which guaranteed they would pay no tax either on the capital gain when sold or on any income from dividends.

14 The Takeover Trail

'That's what a dawn raid is – you hit at dawn' –
Robert Holmes à Court.

Hardly a day goes by when the news headlines do not contain a major story about a takeover. Usually it is one large company bidding a billion-dollar sum for another. Often the bid is unwelcome: that is, the directors and management of the targeted company would rather be left alone. And what normally happens is that the investment bankers or stockbrokers to the predator company send a pre-printed letter, known as an offer document, to the shareholders of the target company, proposing to purchase their shares for cash or for stock in their own corporation, or a mixture of the two.

This inevitably raises the biggest question that arises with any takeover – value. How do you value a public company? One simple answer is market capitalization: the price of each share on the stock markets on a given day multiplied by the number of shares issued. Then all a bidder has to do is to pitch his offer sufficiently higher than the current price in order to persuade shareholders to give up their long-term prospects with the existing board of directors.

But is the stock market price the right one? The prices of shares are fixed not by any measure of assets or even current profits, but by the market's perception of value based on all the information that might affect a company's future cash flow. All the company's financial statements are digested and assessed against competitive forces by scores of analysts. Their collective wisdom is pitted with the judgement of those who make markets and distilled into a share price. This sounds entirely plausible, but how can you then account for the fact that the world stock market as a whole on 19 October 1987 was worth only four-fifths of what it had been the previous day? Or that on the same day ten years later the

FTSE index was three times higher? Share prices can only really be the best guess at a value. An acquirer is not really buying the buildings, machinery and the workforce – he is getting what he thinks these are capable of producing.

As the Wall Street arbitrageur, Ivan Boesky, later to be gaoled for insider trading, put it in 1985:

> An analyst may fully understand a company he is following, may even be able to forecast its future earnings with unmatched precision. Does that mean he can forecast its future stock price with any precision at all? Of course not. Price-earnings multiples averaged as high as 25 or so in the heyday of stock trading in the 1960s. In the mid-seventies these multiples had fallen to 6 and 7. Any stock market price is buffeted by sweeping market forces that are virtually impossible to predict with any reliability. These forces are often important: the growth rate of the economy, the course of interest rates, the international value of the dollar, the inflation rate, an overseas war, a presidential election. They also can be distressingly unimportant: this week's change in money supply, the Federal Reserve Board's sale of securities, its reversal of that sale the next day.

Nevertheless many large and significant public corporations have changed hands on the simple basis of share values. The predators have got what they wanted. The shareholders, presumably, were satisfied because they were able to take a profit and re-invest their money elsewhere. But the companies and their staffs that found themselves with new owners were not necessarily better companies for the transformation. In some cases new blood made them more efficient, and more effective use was made of their assets. 'Making assets sweat' is one of the main justifications for takeovers. In many others the acquiring company, its costs swollen by the expense of its own acquisition, has fallen apart.

I doubt whether there is any better example of this than what happened to Australia's three main television networks in the late eighties. The Nine Network was controlled by Kerry Packer, a single-minded entrepreneur with a reputation for seeking value in his investments and businesses. Run by a New Zealander, Sam Chisholm, later to become managing director of British Sky Broadcasting, it topped viewer ratings year after year. The Seven Network was owned by leading newspaper interests, including the Fairfax dynasty, proprietors of the influential *Sydney Morning Herald* and the *Melbourne Age*. And Network Ten was owned by Rupert Murdoch's family company.

Just before the Great Crash of 1987, Packer sold his network to the ambitious Alan Bond for A$1.1 billion – a figure which represented a premium on its market worth, and was much more than its true value. Another eager entrepreneur with Hollywood ambitions, former financial journalist Christopher Skase, paid A$780 million – well over the odds – for Seven. And, as Australian law prohibits foreign interests controlling the electronic media, Murdoch was forced to sell Network Ten when he took American citizenship. He did so, at a handsome price, to some would-be media moguls who thought commercial television was, as Lord Thomson of Fleet had once put it, 'a licence to print money'.

All three newcomers crashed, their networks flattened not so much by an advertising recession as by the crippling interest rate burden of acquisition. In 1990 Packer bought back his Nine Network for one half of what he had been paid for it. The other two networks went into receivership, and for years were run by banks and firms of accountants. In each case the aspirants had made miscalculations about their future cash flows.

Not all of those carrying out takeovers continue to run the businesses they have bought. In many cases they sell the assets for cash. Asset-stripping became fashionable in the eighties and is a popular occupation of those who believe that the stock markets often underestimate the true value of companies, and they put their beliefs to the test by acquiring businesses and then breaking them up. This has frequently happened in the past when a company has a number of assets on its books – particularly real estate – which have not been written up with inflation. By disposing of the property, or by coming to a lease-back arrangement with a finance company, an asset-stripper can acquire huge sums of cash. By the 1990s the activities of two generations of asset-strippers had sharpened up directors to the risk, though there is still a hard core of professionals on every continent who make money by spotting companies that are under-valued.

Despite the asset-strippers and the ordinary everyday risks

in mergers, such evidence as there is shows that takeovers often succeed in their objective of achieving real growth for the acquiring company. A study published by McKinsey, the management consultancy, found that even cross-border acquisitions had achieved a high rate of success compared with other forms of corporate expansion.

McKinsey reviewed the overseas acquisition programmes of the top 50 companies in Europe, Japan and the United States – and found that 57 per cent were judged a success. However almost all the success stories related to a company merging with another in the same business. Most of those involving moving into non-core businesses failed.

Takeover Rules

In each country there are rules that govern takeovers. In some cases these rules are enshrined in legislation, in others they form part of a code, written or unwritten. In Britain the rules do not have statutory backing and have been rewritten several times since they first appeared as the City Takeover Code in March 1968. Their observation is supervised by the City Takeover Panel, a group of twelve City elders whose modest secretariat is based on the twentieth floor of the Stock Exchange building. There are a director-general, two deputies, a secretary and a few other executives. The permanent staff provide interpretations of the Code, but contested rulings and disciplinary cases are considered by the Panel itself, with the right of appeal to the Appeals Committee, which sits under the chairmanship of a retired Lord of Appeal. The Panel operates under the watchful eye of the Bank of England; it is usual for the majority of its staff to be on secondment from the Bank, providing a constant flow of fresh ideas.

The most important rule is that you may bid for up to 29.9 per cent of a company's shares before launching a full bid, but after that you must make a full offer for all the remaining shares, at the highest price you have paid for the purchases so far. This is to prevent a predator buying a company on the cheap, especially where there is a wide spread of share ownership.

Another fundamental principle is that shareholders must be treated evenly. 'All shareholders of the same class of an offeree company must be treated similarly.' Another rule provides that before an offer is announced, no one privy to the preliminary takeover or merger discussions is allowed to deal in the shares of either the bidding or target company. Once an offer is announced, the share transactions in all the companies involved must be reported by all parties to the City Takeover Panel, the Stock Exchange and the press. Companies defending a bid must not do anything without shareholder approval 'which could effectively result in any bona fide offer being frustrated, or in the shareholders of the offeree company being denied an opportunity to decide on its merits'.

The City Takeover Panel's executive staff are available throughout a takeover to advise whether the rules are in danger of being broken, as all bids for public companies, listed or unlisted, are strictly monitored. The staff work closely with the surveillance unit at the Stock Exchange to investigate dealings in advance of publication of bid proposals, the aim being to establish whether there has been any breach of the rules governing secrecy and abuse of privileged information.

If there appears to have been a breach of the code, the Panel staff invite the chairman of the company involved, or other individuals, to appear before the Panel. He or she is informed by letter of the nature of the alleged breach, and of the matters which the director-general will present to the hearing. These hearings are informal, there are no rules of evidence, and, although notes are taken, no permanent records are kept. The principal against whom the complaint has been made is expected to appear in person, although he may bring his lawyer with him. At the hearing he is expected to set out his reply, normally based on a document which should already have been produced in reply to the director-general's letter. If the Panel finds there has been a breach, the offender may be reprimanded there and then, or may be subjected to public censure with a press release distributed to the media, setting out the Panel's conclusions and its reasons for them. In a bad case, where the Panel feels that the offender should no longer be able to use the Stock Exchange temporarily or permanently, the case may be referred to a professional association, the Stock Exchange, the Department of Trade and Industry, or the City Fraud Squad.

The Panel is considered to be a legal entity, and the Court of Appeal has ruled that its decisions may, if need be, be reviewed by the Courts.

Making an Acquisition

Before considering how a takeover works, it is perhaps worth analysing some of the many and varied reasons for making an acquisition. The most obvious is that it is often much easier and cheaper than starting a new business, except in the case of a product or service that is exclusive enough to depend for its success on the professional drive and energy of the entrepreneur and his team. If you have a product that will put your rivals out of business, you will usually be best served by building up the business yourself.

But if you wish to expand a business, a takeover is a useful route. Apart from anything else, it often enables you to use other people's money to achieve your ambition. A takeover can be a way of swallowing up the competition, and thereby increasing profit margins.

This was the case with many of the large takeovers in the early part of this century, when the first wave of mergers took place. Many of these were designed to set up large monopolies that could raise prices in basic industries such as steel, power and transport. Some of them were brought about by the legendary New York financier, J. Pierpont Morgan. His biggest deal, in 1901, brought together 11 companies that accounted for half of America's steel industry to form US Steel.

These days there are regulations to prevent monopolies through merger. In the United States there are strong antitrust laws, and the European Commission is also vigilant against the development of new monopolies. New European rules effective in September 1990 gave the Brussels-based Commission control over not just the major mergers and acquisitions, but also over small purchases made by mega companies. Mergers are subjected to Commission scrutiny where the combined worldwide turnover of the undertakings involved is more than 5 billion ECU, and where the Community-wide turnover of at least two of the undertakings is above 250 million ECU. Additionally Britain has a Monopolies and Mergers Commission.

In many cases, a takeover may appear to be the only way to fulfil ambitions of growth. Sometimes a takeover may be the result of egomania on the part of the chairman or controlling shareholder; there is never a shortage of new owners for Britain's national newspapers, for instance, or for prestigious department stores, and breweries also seem popular. Sometimes the thrust of a takeover effort is to achieve a lifetime ambition, such as the fruitless attempt by Lord Forte and his son Rocco to gain control of the Savoy Hotel in London.

Whatever the reason, there are usually only two forms of takeover: those that are uncontested, and those that involve a fight. But it is never as simple as that. There have been many occasions when a board of directors has decided to open merger discussions with a potential target rather than to proceed by stealth, only to find that the opposition is so great that all they have achieved is to give the other side advance warning to prepare for an assault. And there have been occasions when a contested battle has been so fierce and the cost of the operation so high that it might have been better to attempt to achieve the same result through negotiation.

Some takeovers are solicited. Many a company, for lack of progress or good management, feels that it would be better served if it were to be incorporated in a better run, and perhaps larger, business. I was once a non-executive director of a small public company in the retail motor trade. It had garages as far-flung as South Wales, Southampton, Birmingham and Lincolnshire, with different franchises in each. In one period of three months the Thatcher government lifted interest rates three percentage points, thereby forcing the sale of used cars in stock at giveaway prices; an oil company decided not to renew the lease on the premises with the best showroom because they wanted a larger forecourt for petrol sales; and a strike at Vauxhall Motors dried up the supply of new cars for valuable orders at the main dealership. The directors, rightly I believe, sought to merge our company with a larger group better able to sit out what was to become a four-year crisis for the motor trade, and entered into discussions with a number of potential buyers. At one stage we were close to a deal. But then our shares slipped in the market; our creditors, seeing our market capitalization falling and rightly assuming that interest bills were rising, pressed harder, and the banks called in the receivers. The irony is that had it been a private company, without a listing, the company could well have weathered the storm, for the shareholders would have been obliged to stick with it through the bad times. Directors, of course, were not allowed to sell out, nor could they tell those friends who had supported the company, because that would have been classed as insider trading, punishable by heavy fines or imprisonment. So those that had risked their savings lost their investment. It seemed rough justice at the time, but does illustrate an important point made earlier: the shareholders in a public company are much better protected than those in a private one.

There may also be hidden hazards in a solicited takeover. Take the case of Sinclair Research, a company built up by a technological wizard, Sir Clive Sinclair, credited with building the world's smallest portable television set, and the designer of an all-British range of microcomputers. Sinclair's drive and technological brilliance were not matched, however, by management skills, and many of his investments, such as his battery-operated vehicle, were less than successful.

In 1983, four years after it was founded, Sinclair Research had a market capitalization of £136 million. In 1983 and 1984 the company was turning in profits of about £14 million, and in 1985, although market conditions turned down due to a slump in the personal computer market, it was still looking to a useful profit. But in May of that year, serious cash-flow problems became evident as stocks of unsold goods valued at £35 million built up, with suppliers demanding payment of their bills. For a while the main creditors, Thorn EMI and Timex of Dundee, agreed to hold off, and Sinclair's bankers, Barclays and Citicorp, increased the company's borrowing facilities. But, almost inevitably, the crunch came, and Sinclair turned to the bear-like clutches of Robert Maxwell, publisher of Mirror Group Newspapers, who, for reasons which have never been made very clear, made a £12 million rescue bid for Sinclair Research. Two months later, on 9 August 1985, it was all off. Maxwell announced that he was pulling out, saying the deal 'just did not gel', though he had no doubt that Sinclair computers were a 'fine product appreciated by millions'. Sir Clive Sinclair put a brave face on it, smiled wanly, and went off to see his creditors. It is a salutary lesson for those who see a takeover as salvation: you have to be sure you are really wanted, or that your saviour is really genuine.

With any takeover there are two stages: the preliminaries, which may take weeks and even months, and the active stage, when the bid is made and the offer digested and voted upon by the shareholders. Very few takeovers are the result of a whim, but are usually considered only after painstaking research, involving the company's solicitors, accountants and merchant banks, or other financial advisers.

Takeover specialists are at a premium in the City, and are paid enormous salaries. A senior director in the corporate finance department of one of the better known British merchant banks may expect to earn about £350,000 a year in salary and bonuses, while a junior director, who could be in his late twenties or early thirties, might receive £100,000 upwards. American companies pay more, but offer marginally less job security. For this, the specialists advise those either making or subject to a takeover on strategy and tactics, capital-raising where necessary, and public relations, often calling in outside specialists to assist.

When the pressure is on, most advisers would expect to work 14 hours a day, as well as attending meetings at weekends. If their homes are outside central London, they would be lucky to see their families except at the weekend, and would almost certainly have to have a flat close to the City. One merchant bank maintains an apartment for its directors above an expensive West End restaurant. However, if you are seen dining with a new client, word soon gets out. Takeover advisers have to work under conditions of great secrecy, for an essential part of the takeover game is to anticipate your opponent's next move, and to outwit him.

However, for the merchant bank that can grab the lion's share of the business, the rewards are great, with takeovers and operations in the European markets earning the greatest portion of its income.

Growth Through Acquisition

In planning a takeover, it is essential to work out a strategy before going public. This usually means weeks closeted with financial advisers, and it is a time when security is all-important. A stray document left in a photocopying machine, a loose word dropped to a friend in a bar, or even a minor indiscretion at lunch can lead to a leak. One paragraph in a newspaper can be enough to set the takeover target's shares racing ahead on the Stock Exchange, which could rule out a bid, or alert rivals to the possibility.

Furthermore, takeover strategy these days is not confined merely to obtaining enough shares in the targeted concern. In almost every situation, politics and public relations come to the fore.

The predator in a takeover enjoys one major advantage: it can always count on the full support of its management team, which usually has much to gain from taking charge of a larger organization. By contrast the management of a target company often finds itself in a difficult, even ambivalent, position; its loyalties are to its present board of directors, but its future, as likely as not, will lie elsewhere. It also has the burden of dealing with a worried staff, not to mention suppliers, distributors, and others with whom the company has close connections. And it has to continue to run the business. It used to be the case that shareholders tended to stand by a business that has done well by them, unless those making the bid make an irrefutable case. But, in 1996, when Rocco Forte tried to persuade shareholders to stick with him, they rejected his pleas and fell for the Irish charm of Gerry Robinson and his Granada group.

It is also true that the best defence against a takeover is to act before a bid, rather than afterwards – in other words, take action which will deter a predator from striking, such as selling off subsidiaries which do not fit the core of the business, or explain the company's strategy to analysts in such a way that the share price rises to reflect an accurate, rather than an undervalued, view of its stock. Once a bid is made, it is hard to do this, because any disposals or other capital restructuring have to be approved by shareholders.

When it is clear that a takeover bid is going to fail, what does the bidder do? There are occasions when a predator can come badly unstuck. Almost certainly he will have built up a parcel of shares in the company in which he is interested, although his bid will be conditional on sufficient acceptances to give him control. No one is expected to make an unconditional bid, but, once the fever is over, it can be difficult to recover the price paid for a block of shares on a rising market, and the bidder may be forced to take a loss. In such cases it is normal to arrange a placement through his brokers, in much the same way as when raising capital for his own concern. It is not unusual for the shares to be picked up by forces sympathetic to the company that has successfully defended itself against takeover, for the last thing directors want is an unstable market, especially if some of the allegations made in the heat of the moment seem likely to have stuck in the minds of the market.

A more interesting development occurs when an unsuccessful bidder actually walks away from the event with a large profit – not uncommon. Sometimes this can be achieved through barefaced cheek, especially if the subject of a bid has a group of directors and a large shareholder determined to hold on to their property at all costs.

This is what happened as a result of a visit on 20 November 1979 by the publisher Rupert Murdoch to his father's old office at the Herald and Weekly Times newspaper group in Melbourne, Australia, where he cheerfully greeted Sir Keith Macpherson, the chairman and chief executive, with the glad tidings that his News Group was about to present the Stock Exchange with the terms of a A$126 million bid for just over half of the company. Since the offer valued Herald and Weekly Times, the country's largest newspaper group, at A$100 million more than News Group, Macpherson suggested that the whole idea was ridiculous.

Perhaps it was; one newspaper later suggested it was like a snake trying to swallow a sheep, and similar metaphors were used when five years later, the entrepreneur, Robert Holmes-Court, made an unsuccessful bid for Australia's largest company, BHP, and was described, colourfully, as 'trying to rape an elephant'. Murdoch, however, knew what he was up to. He wanted the Herald and Weekly Times desperately – ever since his father, whose genius had built up the paper, had died, he had set his sights on it – but he suspected that he would not get it, even though News Group offered A$4 a share, a premium of A$1.26 on the market price.

His suspicions were correct. His bid caused panic at the headquarters of another newspaper group 400 miles away in Sydney. John Fairfax Ltd, a conservative family concern, had a minority stake in Herald and Weekly Times, and its newspapers were bitter rivals of Murdoch's. Apart from the extra power Murdoch would gain if he controlled HWT, he would become a partner of Fairfax in two other major enterprises, Australian Newsprint Mills, the country's only newsprint manufacturer, and Australian Associated Press, the national news agency, both controlled jointly by Fairfax and HWT. Fairfax instructed its brokers to buy all the HWT shares it could muster to thwart Murdoch, and the price rose quickly to well above the A$4 that Murdoch had offered. Within two days Fairfax had laid out over A$50 million and had acquired 15 per cent of HWT. The shares stood at A$5.52. Murdoch knew that he was beaten, but he saw a lucrative way out. Instead of conceding defeat, he instructed his brokers, J. B. Were and Co., to continue buying shares but on a much more limited scale. At the same time he commissioned another broker, May and Mellor, to unload the 3,500,000 shares he had already purchased. The Fairfax people, convinced that Murdoch was still a buyer, snapped up the lot, paying top prices, only to face the humiliation of hearing that they had been outwitted and that Murdoch had quit, using one of his own newspapers to condemn the Fairfax 'rescue' of HWT as 'two incompetent managements throwing themselves into each other's arms at the expense of their shareholders'. Maybe, but the real point was that Fairfax was determined to stop Murdoch at any price, and paid dearly for it – for when the shares settled back down at a lower price, it had lost over A$20 million, plus the interest on the A$50 million laid out to acquire the stock.

Ironically, several years later Murdoch got his prize, as a result of some spectacular blunders by Warwick Fairfax, a junior member of the Fairfax family, whose dealings in the junk bond market lost him the empire his grandfather had built. The trick is that your opponent has to hate the idea of losing his beloved company so much that he will pay almost anything to keep it. It is not a ploy that is encouraged by some of the more conservative bodies in the City of London, but it is fair game, and the best defence, if you are sure that the predator does not have the nerve or the money to go ahead with a bid, is to call his bluff, let him face the test of the market, and then take large advertisements in the financial press to deliver a wounding riposte.

In most contested takeovers the issue of who wins is decided by institutional investors, as the major shareholders. In Britain they are not quite as fickle as in the United States, on which more later, but increasingly the institutions are under pressure to perform. Stanley Kalms, whose Dixons electronics group won control of the electrical goods retailer Currys in 1984, accurately reflected the current attitude: 'Companies can only expect loyalty when their shares are performing well, and the market has confidence in the management.'

The New Takeover Game

'Speculators may do no harm as bubbles on a steady stream of enterprise. But the position is serious when enterprise becomes the bubble on a whirlpool of speculation. When the capital development of a country becomes a by-product of the activities of a casino, the job is likely to be ill done,' wrote John Maynard Keynes in 1936. 'What kind of society isn't structured on greed? The problem of social organization is how to set up an arrangement under which greed will do the least harm,' said Milton Friedman, in 1973.

Those who promote takeovers – or believe that there should be no restriction other than a prohibition on monopoly – argue their case by saying that shareholders benefit by the maximization of share values. They also suggest that business is made more efficient, and necessary rationalization brought about, because large and indolent managements are forced to promote change in order to survive. Be that as it may, the real

reason for the frenzy of takeover activity in Britain and elsewhere is the desire of large numbers of corporate raiders to get
rich.

As is usually the case, the Americans are well ahead when
it comes to exploiting the possibilities available to the corporate raider. Indeed, so sophisticated have US financial markets become that individuals are able to use an array of new
financial instruments to play the same old games. One game,
popular in the mid-nineties, called appropriately 'Copycat',
and involves studying the moves of renowned old-style
raiders like T. Boone Pickens, and emulating them. You will
be 24 hours behind, of course, but those who have followed
this course in a bull market have seldom fared badly. Nor is
there any need to use much of your own money; you can buy
stock options for a fraction of the real cost, exercise the
option when the price rises, and then sell out for a large
capital gain.

It sounds like, and is, the stuff on which the 1929 Wall
Street crash was founded, but now there are record numbers
of people playing the share markets, and using sophisticated
methods to do so. Scores of computer programs have become
available for individuals to analyse their portfolio performances, and to carry out 'what if?' analyses. Some programs
are highly advanced, and can detect prices of related stocks
that get out of step with each other. Armed with his personal
computer and a copy of the *Financial Times*, the personal
investor found he was almost as well informed as many professional investment advisers. There was no need to accept
the low returns offered by his neighbourhood bank, or savings institution. Why should he not get the kind of interest,
or strike the kind of deals, organized by the big boys? He
wanted to climb on to the gravy train.

In 1980 only 49 million shares changed hands daily on the
New York Stock Exchange. By 1991 this had more than
tripled to 156 million shares. In this period prices rose
sharply. Two-thirds of the rise is credited by analysts as being
due to a feverish increase in takeover activity.

Much of this American activity was fuelled by borrowed
money, in which the leveraged takeover has been a favourite
technique. A corporate raider would take a modest position
in a large company, wait a short while, and then offer to buy

the entire stock by making a takeover bid. Where would the corporate raider's small company raise these billions of dollars from, you may well ask. Simple. He would approach a broker specializing in the art of raising junk bonds for worthwhile causes.

Where There's Junk There's Money

The man in the street might suppose that those proposing to take over a company have the wherewithal to do so. After all, takeover merchants have always been painted as piranhas swallowing the small fry. This is not necessarily the case.

In the late 1980s many takeovers were achieved with borrowed money, and in some instances this money was borrowed, indirectly, from the company that the predator was targeting.

Let me explain. Company X wishes to buy company Y, but has insufficient spare cash on its balance sheet to do so. Nor does it have enough security to offer its bankers, and it does not believe it can raise cash from its shareholders in a rights issue.

So instead it issues junk bonds, which are no different from any other interest-bearing security except that they carry a substantially higher than average interest rate. These bonds raise the capital required to finance a bid, and are normally secured against the shares of the company targeted. An investor in a junk bond normally does so on the basis that his money is only committed if the takeover bid succeeds. If it is successful the corporate raider issuing the bond can afford to pay the higher interest rates because he will have the assets of the newly acquired company at his disposal. In other words the strength of the victim company's balance sheet is its own downfall. If the corporate raider fails and is unable to get enough shares in his target, it is a fair bet they will have risen in the market, and he will have made a sizeable capital gain.

The use of junk bonds was championed most heavily in the 1980s by the Wall Street broking firm Drexel Burnham Lambert, where its greatest advocate was Michael Milken. By 1985 $27 billion worth of junk bonds had been issued, most of them through Drexels. In 1970 there had been only

$7 billion worth of high-yield bonds outstanding, and most of that was for quality offerings. By 1989, at the peak of the junk bond craze, $201 billion of junk had been unloaded.

Many people imagine that the holders of junk were avaricious investors, dissatisfied with the more prosaic returns available on ordinary investments. They were not. At the beginning of 1989, 30 per cent of junk bonds outstanding in the United States were held by insurance companies, 30 per cent by mutual funds, and 15 per cent by pension funds. Many of them lost their money as the companies in which the junk was secured turned down. Drexels went bankrupt, and Michael Milken went to gaol. Junk bonds went out of fashion.

Poison Pills

There were other forces at work in the leveraged takeover game which have caused grave disquiet, particularly for those who subscribe to the old-fashioned view that since a public company is owned by its shareholders it is reasonable to assume that their interests take precedence. The truth, of course, is a little different.

Lord Hanson. In its heyday more than half of Hanson Trust's income came from businesses in the United States. In August 1985, Hanson identified a major American company as a suitable case for takeover. The SCM Corporation was a solid if dreary conglomerate which manufactured outmoded typewriters, processed food, pigments and an assortment of other products. On 21 August, Hanson Trust offered $60 a share in cash for SCM Corporation, valuing the company at $755 million, well below its market capitalization. Robert Morton, an analyst with brokers de Zoete and Bevan, told me at the time that this was 'in the mould of Hanson acquisitions: SCM is exactly the kind of company he goes for, a company which has already undergone a great deal of rationalization and sorting out, which perhaps has not been fully realized by the shareholders.'

The SCM management was horrified. Here was this lord from England buying their company at rock-bottom value. By all the precedents, it was clear that, before they knew where they were, they would be looking for new jobs. Fortunately for them the board saw matters the same way, rejected the Hanson bid, and refused even to talk to Hanson's US chief Sir Gordon White, despite several invitations to do so. It hastily called in its financial advisers, the New York firm of Goldman Sachs.

Curiously, however, it was not Goldman Sachs that came to the rescue of SCM's beleaguered management, but Wall Street's largest broking house, the New York financial conglomerate Merrill Lynch. Merrill Lynch's capital markets division, headed by a young go-getter, Ken Miller, was hungry for new business, and skilful in organizing what has become known as leveraged management buyouts. Within a few days, Miller and his team had come up with a means whereby, at the stroke of a pen, Hanson could be thwarted, the SCM management could save their jobs, and Merrill Lynch would receive a large fee.

So it was that on 30 August, only nine days after Hanson's bid, a new company was announced – legally a partnership between the SCM Corporation's management and Merrill Lynch, but funded by the Prudential Assurance Company of America. It offered $70 a share – $10 more than Hanson – for 85 per cent of the SCM shares, and promised to buy the rest out of SCM profits at some future date, through the issue of junk bonds, which, it was hoped, would trade at about $70. A confidential Merrill Lynch paper described the deal as representing 'one of the most asset-rich LBO opportunities we have ever encountered'.

The wily Merrill Lynch team hoped that Lord Hanson would withdraw, but they took sensible steps to protect themselves, and their fees, if he did not. If Miller pulled this one off it would be the first time that a leveraged management buyout had been successful against a tender offer for cash. But there was a risk, so a clause was written into the contract providing for a $9 million fee should the bid be topped and the arrangement terminated, in addition to the basic fee of £1.5 million for fixing the deal in the first place.

Lord Hanson proved their fears justified. On 3 September, Hanson Trust increased its offer to $72 a share. Unlike the first offer, which valued SCM at a bargain basement price, this was a much more attractive offer for shareholders. For a start it was all in cash, with no waiting around for junk bonds and future profits which might or might not appear. For the SCM management, however, it presented the same problem, the prospect of losses, made even more certain as a result of their tactics in signing up with Merrill Lynch, and handing over $9 million of the company's money in fees. Sir Gordon White did, however, hold out an olive branch. On 10 September, after several failed attempts by telephone to contact SCM's chairman or board, he sent them one further invitation: 'We believe it is in our mutual interests, including those of your stockholders, management and employees, that we should meet promptly.'

There was no reply, for, behind the scenes, Miller and his team had again been hard at work, advancing another, much more ruthless, way of frustrating Hanson's ambitions. Meanwhile the $9 million fee had already been placed in escrow. The new plan was to strip out of SCM Corporation its two most potentially profitable businesses, in the belief that the Englishman would either lose interest or be left with a crippled business.

This tactic has become known as the use of the 'poisoned pill', although a more appropriate metaphor might be that of a scorched earth policy. In this instance, the SCM management and Merrill Lynch increased their leveraged buyout offer to $74 a share, but subjected it to a new condition: if Hanson or another party got more than a third of SCM shares, Merrill would have the right to purchase the two most thriving parts of the SCM Corporation – the pigments and processed food businesses – at knockdown prices. The business would then be run by the same SCM management. These two businesses were to become known as the 'crown jewels', for Merrill Lynch obtained the options for a total of $430 million against the SCM board's own valuation of $400 million for the pigments business and $90 million for the foods division. For organizing this neat new arrangement, Merrill Lynch took a retention fee of $6 million, investment banking fees of $8m., and dealer-manager fees of $2.75 million, in addition, of course, to the $11.5 million already paid.

The next morning Hanson Trust withdrew its $72 a share offer, and spent $200 million buying SCM shares on the New York market; within a few hours it had acquired 25 per cent of the company. But on 16 September Merrill Lynch acted again. With the Manufacturers Hanover Bank working as agent, it put the shares of the crown jewel subsidiaries in escrow, and apparently beyond Hanson's reach. At this point the lawyers took over, with the action moving to the New York District Court in Lower Manhattan. In the end Hanson Trust lost the case, but the verdict was reversed in the subsequent appeal.

Discussion in the United States has ranged over whether the law courts are really the place to decide such matters, as well as whether the frenzy of takeover activity wastes scarce investment capital, inhibits innovation, and forces managers to sacrifice long-term goals to the next quarterly profits sheet. Kathryn Rudie Harrigan, Professor of Strategic Management at the Columbia University Business School, talked to me about the increasingly common tendency for stock market takeovers to be decided in courts of law:

> It is just one more in a string of devices that managers and their investments bankers have come up with to avoid being taken over when they do not want to be.

Is this new trend likely to be damaging to shareholders? Professor Harrigan thinks perhaps not, in that values are often forced up by what is essentially a game:

> It is a game, and it is a game that is played with great ritual, and is being played in many, many companies these days. It is often cheaper to acquire something than it is to build it from the ground up.

But she does believe that business will suffer in the end:

> I think it is damaging to the long-term health of the business, because when you are so busy satisfying these short-term requests of the financial community, who are looking for instant gratification from their investment, you often cripple the long-term ability of the company to be able to reposition itself to remain competitive in a changing environment.

Professor Harrigan also believes that the concepts of poison pills and crown jewels could be exported to Britain:

The two capital markets are becoming very similar in the way that people operate within them, and the kinds of expectations they have of the companies whose equities they hold. And more and more of the equities are held by institutional investors, who have this kind of short-term expectation, and they want to see this quick pay-off on their investment. I think the kind of behaviour we see here, with these leveraged buyouts, will undoubtedly be appearing also in your stock markets.

'Abuses by some banks and financiers are feeding a take-over frenzy that strikes at the economic well-being of this country,' one potential victim of a leveraged takeover wrote to Paul Volcker, then the chairman of the Federal Reserve. 'They are engaging in stock and bond and credit schemes reminiscent of those of the 1920s – but on a multi-billion dollar scale.' By extending the 50 per cent rule to shell companies, Volcker did not rule out using such tactics. He just made them less attractive – 50 per cent less attractive, in fact. For those that have the stamina to engage in it, it is still potentially a high-risk strategy, so long as you can stay ahead of the game.

15 Policing the Markets

'The financial planning industry is in many ways still in the days of the Wild West. The marshal hasn't ridden into town, there's mayhem in the streets, a lot of random shooting' – Scott Stapf of the North American Securities Administrators' Association.

'Unless investigators can uncover a tape recording with irrefutable evidence that Box told Cox to "fill your boots", they are banging their heads against a well-fortified wall of self-interest which inevitably protects those who have made a fortune by being ahead of the game' – editorial in the British newspaper, *Sunday Business*.

At four o'clock in the morning of 23 October 1812, three men called at the Popincourt Barracks in Paris with the devastating news that the Emperor Napoleon had died beneath the walls of Moscow. It was a plausible story – news from the campaign front took three weeks to get back and the French armies had just achieved a great victory at the Battle of Borodino that had opened the gates to the Russian capital. The men also said that the Senate had abolished the Empire and appointed a Provisional Government, and was calling on the 10th Cohort of the National Guard for support. Within hours a huge conspiracy against Napoleon was under way, and the Emperor's leading supporters were thrown into prison.

This story, told in more recent times by Italian author, Guido Artom, in his book *Napoleon is Dead in Russia*, was the inspiration for one of Britain's most notorious examples of share-market rigging. In the early nineteenth century only major news moved the fledgling stock market, and it took headlines like 'Napoleon Set to Invade', or, better still, 'Napoleon Dead' to move the market.

Since, even in the days before the telegraph, old news was no news, so stockbrokers often placed faithful retainers in the port of Dover to listen to the rumour mill, watch the sea, talk to fishermen, and report back regularly. So, when on 21 February 1814, Colonel de Burgh, alias Charles Random de Bérenger, turned up in Dover in a red uniform, saying he was aide de camp to General Lord Cathcart, and reported the death of Napoleon and the fall of Paris, the news reached London at the speed of a pony and trap. Although foreign reporting was severely limited in those days, along with share ownership, there were those in London who had heard of the earlier, unsuccessful conspiracy against Napoleon, and the subsequent execution, not only of the plotters, but also of the soldiers who unwittingly carried the message. They were therefore very much on their guard against such stories. But 'Colonel de Burgh' had an elaborate cover story, a detailed account of how Napoleon had been butchered by the Cossacks. He had also made a point of going directly to the headquarters of the Port Admiral in Dover to apprise him of the facts. Surely, said brokers, it must be true.

Prices on the Stock Exchange shot up, as the wealthy clients of brokers received the news, apparently confirmed by hand bills distributed in the streets of London. They were not to know that these had also been handed out by de Bérenger who had himself taken a coach to the capital, to collect his gains, estimated at about £10,000. It was, of course, all pure fiction, but note that those who lost out were those who had been contacted by brokers, those who, themselves, were often privileged possessors of inside information, which, in this case, turned out to be false.

Not much changed in the following 175 years. Until recently it was those 'in the know' who stood to make rich pickings from speculative trading on the Stock Exchange. Latter-day frauds on similar lines to that perpetrated by de Bérenger were common in the early 1970s, during the so-called Australian mining boom. Reports of a nickel 'strike' by an obscure, barely known and usually recently listed mining company would reach Sydney as a result of a tip from Kalgoorlie, a remote dusty gold town in Western Australia. Confirmation was impossible, but the word flashed round, and the price of the stock shot up. I once worked on a magazine where the financial editor would return from lunch, very excited, and shout something like 'Bosom's Creek has struck nickel', and rush to the phone to buy shares. Some brokers made a point of reserving shares for journalists, who could be counted upon to write favourably about a mining prospect, which, more often than not, when the geologists' report arrived, turned out to be nothing more than a hole in the ground or a stick marking a spot in the desert. Fortunes were made and lost.

Much of the activity was 12,000 miles from the geologists' trowels. Each day, as soon as the London Stock Exchange opened there was feverish activity as investors sought to cash in. Many had their fingers badly burned, and the two-year 'boom' earned Australian brokers a bad reputation which took years to live down. As one merchant banker, who frequently visits Sydney, put it: 'The Aussies saw it as a way of getting their own back on the Poms.'

Ramping stocks was not confined to those on the fringe of share markets. Writing in the *Observer* on 5 September 1971, under the headline 'Digging up the Dirt', I reported how an Australian Senate Committee investigation into the series of mining collapses and false claims in that country had severely shaken investors' confidence.

One thoroughly dishonest practice disclosed to the Committee was the purchase of huge blocks of shares in early trading by certain brokers, using their house accounts. By lunchtime, word would be round the markets that a particular share was on the move, and the broking house would unload its newly acquired holding at a substantial profit. Those shares that remained unsold would be allocated to clients for whom the firm held discretionary accounts, at a substantially higher price than the firm had paid for them, thereby enabling it to take a profit at its clients' expense. To add insult to injury, the clients would be charged brokerage, but usually would be none the wiser, for they would see from the *Australian Financial Review* that they had apparently obtained the shares at the 'market price'.

The Committee's report makes interesting reading, even years after the inquiry. It scrutinized in detail the accounts of one sharebroking firm that had gone into liquidation, only to find that about 80 per cent of the firm's trading was on its own account, and that its income from commission amounted to only a minor proportion of turnover.

Another prominent Sydney stockbroker, who was also a director of two major mining companies, was exposed for trying to have one of the companies taken over by a joint venture operation, in which his stockbroking firm's affiliated investment house had a stake. Evidence to the Senate Committee revealed that the stockbroker planned the takeover without informing the company chairman or his fellow directors, and that an associate company of his firm was to act as the underwriters.

Let us move back to London, and to Wednesday 13 June 1985. It was a typical summer Thursday on the Stock Exchange. Trading was languid, as is so often the case at this time of the year. Then came a sudden burst of activity, much to the curiosity of a party from a Norfolk Women's Institute that was visiting the public gallery that day. Someone was buying large blocks of shares in Arthur Bell and Sons plc, and their prices rose by 14 per cent.

The visitors had to wait until reading their Saturday edition of the *Eastern Daily Press* to find out why. Guinness plc had made a bid for Bell on Friday the 14th, and on the eve of that takeover offer, someone had got wind of what was going on, and had been buying Bell's shares furiously in the hope of a quick profit. Yet 'insider trading' is strictly forbidden both by the law, which since 1980 has made it a criminal offence, and by the rules of the Stock Exchange. Despite that, as a practice, it is still widespread.

According to the magazine *Acquisitions Monthly*, the share prices of takeover targets rise on average between 20 and 30 per cent in the month before a bid. Over 90 per cent of prices move before a bid. One reason for this may well be that astute investors have spotted, from their own research, likely targets for takeover. Passing insider information is more likely.

To combat this the Stock Exchange maintains a special squad of men and women at its Throgmorton Street offices to try to track down insider traders. This means questioning those suspected of using inside knowledge to make money, and putting the evidence before the Exchange's Disciplinary Committee.

New and powerful computers allow the squad to spot erratic price movements in London and on other major international markets, and they have the authority to question anyone who works for a member of the Stock Exchange, which, of course, includes a large number of international banks and other financial conglomerates. Their computers have instant access to all Stock Exchange transactions over the previous six months, and they may manipulate the database by asking over 100 questions.

But just like detectives from the regular police forces, they rely more on hot tips from informants than the craftsmanship of a Sherlock Holmes. The number of tips runs at about ten a week. Many of them come from market makers spotting something suspicious. Since market makers can lose thousands of pounds by incorrect pricing, they are very aware of phoney figures.

The Stock Exchange also has the backing of compliance officers employed in securities houses. These men and women make sure that both the Stock Exchange rules and their own house rules on share trading are strictly observed, and if they spot an irregularity in a transaction involving another firm, they usually report it to their opposite number.

Some companies are stricter than others in observing the code of conduct they insist staff must obey when buying and selling stock on their own account. Chase Securities insists that all transactions are placed through the company, and that compliance staff are notified. At most securities houses the phone transactions of all dealing staff are logged, so that investigators could, if they wished, find out who telephoned whom and when. Some firms have taken this a stage further and record the telephone calls of all staff.

A mixture of recorded conversations and the alertness of the London Stock Exchange's surveillance unit has already been responsible for trapping several insider traders. Just before the Mecca group bid for Pleasurama, the casinos and restaurant company, the members of the unit spotted that there had been an increasing amount of trading in Pleasurama. Their suspicions were further aroused when they received calls from market makers in some leading broking firms drawing their attention to the fact that something irregular must be going on. Compliance officers at several houses were phoned, and after a tape at Morgan Grenfell had been played, it was discovered that a tip had been passed on by a female member of Samuel Montagu's corporate finance team. This was the department involved in advising Mecca on its offer. The other banks then listened to their own tape recordings, and the woman plus two others who had used the information were unceremoniously sacked. The three stood to have made a useful sum of money from trading on inside information. That they were caught owes much to their own greed and the vigilance of the surveillance squad. If they had been more cautious and less avaricious their dealings might well have passed unnoticed.

Even so, many insider traders escape detection. One particular problem is the use of nominee companies in offshore tax havens as the trading vehicle. The Stock Exchange team of former policemen, computer consultants, stockbrokers and accountants, say they often follow good leads only to come up against obstacles when a block of shares is purchased by a nominee company. 'There is no way we can see at the moment of busting offshore companies without international cooperation,' I was told. 'All the old names are always there – the Cayman Isles and so on. But it is not only in the Caribbean or in Liberia that this problem exists – much closer to home, in the Channel Islands or the Isle of Man we have just no hope of getting behind the nominee thing.'

At the time of writing it is 15 years since the notorious Guinness scandal, but insider trading is still rife and largely undetected, even in very major takeover bids involving corporations of the highest reputation. Ahead of an announcement in September 1999 by the Natwest banking group that it intended to bid for the Legal and General insurance group, the latter's price shot up by 10 per cent in value as 41 million shares changed hands in a single day. The Stock Exchange announced the inevitable inquiry, and there were rebukes to the adviser banks, Schroders and JP Morgan, but as *Sunday Business* said there did not 'seem a hope in hell of tracking down the culprits: by mid-afternoon on Thursday even the shoe-shine boy on Liverpool Street station knew that L and G was a takeover target'. The newspaper commented of this sequel to the Guinness affair:

That extraordinary affair, which resulted in jailings and a swath of new rules and regulations, was supposed to have marked a turning point in stock market ethics. But for all the huffing and puffing of high-minded governments and handsomely-rewarded City regulators, the age-old practice of trading on 'well sourced' information is as prevalent today as it was in the go-go 1980s.*

The Securities and Exchange Commission

Policing the markets is conducted in two ways: through self-regulation by quasi-official bodies set up by stock exchanges in consultation with governments, or by official agencies staffed by professionals. For many years there have been arguments about which is the more effective way of protecting the investor and preventing fraud and corruption. The debate continues, but, with time and experience, the weight of opinion seems to be moving in favour of a regulatory system run by full-time professionals with no vested interest in any company within the securities industry.

The most important regulatory body in the world is the United States Securities and Exchange Commission (SEC), which protects the interests of America's estimated 50 million investors. Although its authority is technically limited to policing the securities industry in the United States, its tentacles are spread much wider, extending, for example, to the conduct of American investment institutions in their operations outside the country.

The SEC, with a staff of 1,800, was established in July 1935, some years after the Wall Street crash of 1929. A Congressional investigation found that there had been stock manipulation on a huge scale, blatant dishonesty and insider trading, and the SEC was established with sweeping powers over the securities industry.

Now all corporations have to file quarterly financial returns, and much more detailed annual ones, with the SEC, as well as informing it promptly of any facts or important events which might affect the market for the company's

---

Sunday Business, 5 September 1999.

stock. Federal laws require companies intending to raise money by selling their own securities to file with the Commission true facts about their operations. The Commission has power to prevent or punish fraud in the sale of securities, and is authorized to regulate stock exchanges. The law under which it operates lays down precise boundaries within which directors, officers and large shareholders may deal in the stock of their companies.

In its time the SEC has notched up some notable successes in prosecuting corporate crime. In August 1968, it filed charges of securities fraud against 14 Merrill Lynch officers and employees. In the end Merrill Lynch publicly consented to an SEC finding that it had used advance inside information from the Douglas Aircraft Company for the advantage of preferred institutional clients, defrauding the investing public of an estimated $4.5 million in the process – no mean sum at the time. The Securities and Exchange Commission is a mecca for bright young lawyers who wish to make their name as determined investigators, and then, as often as not, get out into lucrative private practice with the SEC name on their credentials.

However, while the SEC has a reputation as a vigorous force, and has claimed many scalps, it is severely constrained in its activities by a shortage of funds. Although the SEC collects fees from registered investment advisers, it has to hand over a large share of the proceeds to the United States Treasury. It has only about 300 enforcement officers to cover the whole of the United States, and the section which deals with the investment management and mutual funds industry has an inspectorate of only about 60 people.

Although this group undertakes about 1,500 spot checks each year on investment advisers, it is not surprising that many confidence tricksters escape unscathed. Officially there are about 17,000 registered investment advisers in the United States, so on average each gets a spot check once a decade, during which time many will have sold their businesses on. But these figures include only the registered advisers. The Consumer Federation of America (CFA) believes that there could be about half a million people acting as unofficial financial advisers, while even the Securities Administrators Association accepts that there are 250,000. Many of these not only claim to offer investment advice; some of them actually manage clients' money.

The SEC also depends greatly on a number of self-regulatory bodies to fulfil its task. For the most part stock exchanges police the activities of their members, and each has an investigations branch. The New York Stock Exchange, the American Stock Exchange and the National Association of Securities Dealers (NASDAQ) all work in close cooperation with the SEC.

The SEC has much wider powers than Britain's Department of Trade, and has much more inclination to use them. The DTI so far has been reluctant to use its power to force open bank accounts and to demand documents, though this may change. But the SEC may subpoena individuals and companies in the US, and demand sight of their bank accounts. Outside America it has agreements with the British, Japanese, Swiss, Cayman Isles and other governments to gather information, and it can also call for sanctions to be imposed on the US branches of un-cooperative foreign banks. Offenders may not only be prosecuted, with penalties as high as three times the illicit profits, but the SEC will turn over all the evidence it has gained to civil litigants who have been disadvantaged as a result of someone's insider trading.

Even these powers are inadequate when one considers the definition of the modus operandi of an insider trader provided by the *Financial Times*:

The would-be insider trader gets a job with the corporate finance department of a merchant bank active in mergers and acquisitions. Always travelling via a third country, he visits two tax havens, Panama and Liechtenstein, which have resisted foreign pressure on their secrecy laws. In each country he sets up a trading company, and opens bank accounts in two or three banks in their names. He only uses banks with no operations or assets in Britain or the United States. He never tells the banks his real name, but arranges for them to deal through a large London broking firm whenever they receive coded instructions over the telephone.

When he picks up inside information, he always trades alone using a call box. He never trades in large amounts, but may break up a transaction into a series of deals from different accounts. He avoids the mistake of trading just before a bid announcement – it makes the market makers vengeful.

As the *Financial Times* pointed out, the SEC's achievements highlighted 'the passivity of the DTI'.

Curiously, though, it was the SEC's biggest coup, catching Boesky, the self-styled 'king of the arbs', that provided the DTI with some of their best leads into City fraud this side of the Atlantic.

Boesky was brought to book because of the Levine case. Levine pleaded guilty, paid back $12.6 million in illegal profits, and talked to the SEC, implicating Boesky. Boesky was charged with making a personal killing on insider information provided by Levine, fined $100 million, barred for life from working on Wall Street, and ordered to dismantle his $2 billion firm.

Boesky was one of the biggest and best-known speculators in the feverish takeover business in America, using a phenomenal network of contacts to make huge profits through arbitraging. Like Levine, he also 'cooperated with the authorities', which is a euphemism for becoming a supergrass in order to keep out of jail.

The Securities and Investment Board

As the millennium approached, Britain was moving towards a sensible regulatory system, not dissimilar to the United States's SEC. It was a hard road, because during the last two decades of the twentieth century practitioners in the financial services industry thought they could create a workable system depending on self-regulation.

The City had grown up on the principle that those in key positions could be trusted. 'My Word is My Bond' was the Stock Exchange motto, and although insider trading was rife, it was true that a handshake sealed a deal. But as the financial markets became more sophisticated, there was concern at two levels – that consumers were being sold products and services that either they did not want or which were unsuited to their financial needs, and that City insiders were making unreasonable profits from their inside information.

An inquiry under Professor Jim Gower was appointed to investigate the need for regulating and policing financial services, and did an extremely thorough job. It found much in the American Securities and Exchange Commission to its liking, and made a series of complicated recommendations. The British government's response to the Gower report and all the lobbying that accompanied it was a classic British fudge which was to remain in place for more than 15 years. The Conservatives led by Margaret Thatcher were ideologically opposed to the creation of a new bureaucracy but also knew that trusting in a handshake was no longer enough to stop people being cheated.

The government wanted the City to police itself – and, in spite of Professor Gower's misgivings – believed it could. But Whitehall decided an umbrella organization was needed to oversee this self-policing, so the Securities and Investment Board was created, staffed by professionals and headed by a former civil servant, Sir Kenneth Berrill. The SIB sat on top of a plethora of self-regulatory bodies – one of which was the Stock Exchange – and tried to make sure they drew up rule books and made their members stick to the rules.

The result was an octopus with tentacles that touched every aspect of the financial services industry, and a set of regulations that were so complex that even the regulators were thoroughly confused. Many of the self-regulatory bodies had names based on hideous acronyms, such as LAUTRO (Life Assurance and Unit Trust Regulatory Organization), IMRO (Investment Management Regulatory Organization), and FIMBRA (Financial Intermediaries, Managers and Brokers Regulatory Organization). The Securities Association was created to take over the regulatory role of the Stock Exchange.

The Securities and Investment Board and these bodies had to follow a number of guidelines laid down by the Financial Services Act. For example, approved investment businesses had to be 'competent, financially sound and to offer best advice' after 'getting to know' the customer.

Berrill could have chosen to leave the definitions vague, and trust the self-regulatory bodies to interpret the law in a reasonable way. Instead, rather in the manner of an American contracts lawyer who anticipates that everything in a deal will go wrong, he drew up very detailed rules, so there could be no ambiguity about what was permissible.

The result was that practitioners had to face some of the most extensive, expensive and taxing conditions imposed on any sector of industry. Whereas the American Declaration of Independence ran to only 1,337 words, and the ten commandments to a mere 333 words, the rule books of SIB and the self-regulatory organisations ran to more than a million words.

It was not long before this panoply of regulation was severely tested, and found wanting, in what became known as the Barlow Clowes affair. In the summer of 1988, thousands of investors reading their daily newspapers were startled to discover that the money they had set aside for pensions or other long-term savings had vanished. Barlow Clowes, the company to which it had been entrusted, was being liquidated. This might, in the history of personal investment, be a familiar story, but what made matters worse was that most of the funds lost were commuted lump sums from life savings or redundancy payments. A majority of the investors were elderly.

What was also particularly interesting about this scandal was that it embroiled both financial advisers and the government. It was not just a question of investors losing their savings as a result of sharp practice by a fund management group. Many of the 11,000 who lost a major part of their life savings did so after being advised to invest in the Barlow Clowes fund by professional independent financial advisers who should have known better. Their defence was that Barlow Clowes had been licensed by the Department of Trade and Industry after suspicions had been raised about the firm's activities.

Barlow Clowes was built up as a low-cost management group. Its funds were not designed to attract the reckless, but the cautious investor seeking a better return than a deposit account in a bank or building society. The attraction was that expert managers would consolidate investors' cash into interest-bearing deposits, principally British gilt-edged securities. That indeed was the intention of the fund's chairman, Peter Clowes, but, alas, he succumbed to the temptation of using some of the cash along the way for sumptuous living, including yachts and fast cars. The sorry tale finally ended in the criminal courts. Peter Clowes spent a number of years in prison, and the regulators had learned the lesson that even the thickest of rule books do not prevent investors being fleeced.

Widespread concern about the complexity of the regulatory system led to Sir Kenneth Berrill being replaced by David Walker, a former executive of the Bank of England, who simplified structures and, while relaxing some aspects of regulation, toughened up others. Even so there continued to be continuous concern about the efficiency of self-regulation, and in 1996 and 1997 a series of pensions scandals came to light. These scandals were not, like Barlow Clowes, examples of blatant fraud, but the product of the uncaring and greedy salesmen from well-known life assurance companies. Incentivized by large commissions, these salesmen persuaded middle-aged people to relinquish their income-based pensions for mone-value schemes, where the total worth varies according to the price of the securities that make up the portfolio. Many people were persuaded to make the change, with the result that most of them could expect a large downturn in their potential pension incomes. This led to many of the companies being fined, and forced to retrain salesforces, as indicated earlier with the example of the Prudential.

When Tony Blair's revitalized Labour Party was elected to government in 1997 one of the first acts was to announce the establishment of an American-style SEC to be known as the Financial Services Authority and intended to be a 'world class regulator'. Headed by a former deputy governor of the Bank of England, Howard Davies, the FSA took over banking regulation from the Bank of England, and integrated the work of the Securities and Investments Board and all its subsidiary self-regulatory organizations. When Davies met the former chairman of the American Federal Reserve Board, Paul Volcker, the big American greeted him with a laugh and the comment: 'Big job, I just hope you can retain your sense of humour.'

The aims of the FSA are clear enough and defined by law:
- *market confidence*: maintaining market confidence in the financial system;
- *public awareness*: promoting public understanding of the financial system;

- *consumer protection*: securing the appropriate degree of protection for consumers;
- *reduction of financial crime*: reducing the extent to which it is possible for a business carried on by a regulated person to be used for a purpose connected with financial crime.

The FSA is politically accountable through the Treasury, which appoints the chairman and the board, which must have a majority of non-executive directors. It has to provide Parliament with an annual report, and hold an annual public meeting. There is also a committee of non-executive board members with clearly defined responsibilities, including ensuring the economic and efficient use of the FSA's resources and setting the pay of executive board members.

One of the most controversial aspects of the FSA's new powers is its role in informing and educating the public. There are those who feel this is not the job of a regulator. Others argue, and I share the view, that given the poor record of the stockbroking community and the City generally in this area, it is good that someone has been delegated the task formally. Even before the organization was formally set up, the body established to foreshadow it had already done some valuable work in this area. It consulted on and published a Consumer Education Strategy which concentrated on education for financial literacy and the provision of consumer education and advice. It set up a Consumer Education Forum to provide the FSA with advice on its consumer education strategy and work programme; published a series of guides for consumers, for example on financial advice and pensions, and established a single point of enquiries for consumers, which deals with up to 2,000 telephone calls a week.

Though politically accountable, the FSA has been given a raft of powers. These include information-gathering powers, powers to require firms to make regular returns or notify particular events, powers to commission expert reports – for example from accountants – and arrangements for direct reporting to the regulator by a firm's auditor or actuary.

But the body says it will not be heavy handed or bureaucratic, preferring to develop a risk-based approach to supervision. As part of this risk-based approach, it says it seeks to 'focus regulatory attention on those firms and activities likely to pose the greatest risk to consumers and markets'.

The FSA has two main investigation powers. The first allows it to conduct general investigation of the affairs of an authorised person and its group, where there is good reason for doing so. The second will allow investigations into a wide range of matters where there is the suspicion that particular offences have been committed or provisions of the Act breached. The FSA can also go to court for a warrant enabling the police to enter and search premises in support of these investigative powers.

As this edition went to press the Financial Services Authority's powers were further enhanced by the British government taking the decision to transfer to it the regulatory powers of the London Stock Exchange. The exchange officially lost its powers as a result of its decision to incorporate as a public company, but the move announced by Gordon Brown, the Chancellor of the Exchequer, also followed several years of criticism.

One of these criticisms surrounded the failure of the exchange to create a suitable regulatory environment for the smaller companies, concentrating its firepower on the FTSE 100 companies that dominate the market. The example of the weakness of the Alternative Investment Market (AIM) compared with the proven success of the Neuer Markt in Germany is cited by critics. Others, though, fear that enlarging the FSA's role still further will lead to its expansion into a large bureaucracy.

Compensation and the Ombudsman

A new compensation scheme provides compensation if an authorised firm is unable to meet its liabilities to investors, depositors or policyholders. The scheme is being operated by a company separate from the FSA, but accountable to it. The authority says its aim is 'to provide a reasonable level of compensation to individual customers and small businesses that have suffered loss as a result of the collapse of a bank, building society, insurer or investment firm'. This is a good idea because it is simpler than the five-scheme system it replaced, providing a single point of entry for consumers.

The same principal has been applied in setting up the Financial Services Ombudsman (FSO), which replaces eight separate ombudsman schemes. As with the compensation scheme, it is being run by a separate company which will be legally and operationally independent of the FSA but will be required to report annually to it on the discharge of its functions.

16   The Global Money Game

'Not only can investors buy and sell stocks and bonds from all over the world, not only can they now do that buying and selling from their home computers, but Internet brokerage sites are now giving them – for free – the information and analytical tools to make those trades, without ever having to call a broker . . .' Thomas Friedman, author of *The Lexus and the Olive Tree*, 1999.

'We have at time a joyless economy' – Warren Bennis, chairman of the Leadership Institute at the University of Southern California.

'You can't have a few people with billions and billions with nothing. That's not a safe situation' – Ted Turner.

The stock markets have come full circle. What started out as a means of financing great global shipping and trading ventures and then slipped into a narrow and more limited mostly national focus is now at the hub of the great global money game. Money moves in seconds to wherever it is most valued. Whether it is a huge fund management group like Fidelity, a billionaire international investor like George Soros or Warren Buffett, or a grandmother in Eastbourne, no one wants their assets located somewhere where they might dissipate overnight, or fall substantially in value. People seek the best returns, whether it be millionaire speculators or timid savers scanning the high street for the best building society. Those with most at stake review their positions constantly and are in a state of readiness to act. Those with modest savings tend to opt for modest but safe returns. Only the mugs ignore the world about them.

That does not mean that large institutions and the super

rich cannot be caught out. This is precisely what happened on 8 December 1997, when the government of Thailand announced it was closing 56 of the country's 58 top private banks. There was an immediate global panic as investors realised that the baht would crash, and that those who had invested in Thailand would lose up to half the value of their investments. The panic spread throughout Asia like a bush fire, and within minutes shares were sliding throughout the region. It became known as the Asian meltdown, the most serious crash for ten years.

Thailand's neighbour, Malaysia, was one of the worst-affected countries, but there the iconoclastic and ascerbic Prime Minister, Mahathir, blamed the crisis on Western speculators. In the capital, Kuala Lumpur, Mahathir's followers burned an effigy of Soros, blaming him for the collapse of the ringit. What Soros had done was, sensibly, to sell the ringit because he believed it to be overvalued.

In the Chinese city of Hong Kong, handed over by the British in a ceremony of pompous optimism only two months earlier, the city's Hang Seng index lost almost one-fifth of its value. The Chinese governor of the former colony appealed for common sense and calm, his words almost a replica of those used by his British counterpart ten years earlier. In Johannesburg, Trevor Manuel, the finance minister, and Chris Stals, then governor of the Reserve Bank of South Africa, stood by wringing their hands as the Johannesburg Stock Exchange shed all its gains of the previous year. In two hours it saw its biggest one-day loss in nine years, sending panic through the bond and currency markets. This was despite a heroic economic performance by the Mandela government whose brave decisions had led to a huge fall in inflation and a steadily improving economy.

Although emerging markets were hit harder by the 1997 turmoil than the established markets of New York, London and Tokyo, no investor was immune from the sudden downturn. The more sensible of them realized, of course, that the correction was just that – a temporary halt to the onward march of the world's share markets, not a crash wiping out long term the value of sound and well-run corporations. Within three months the major markets had not only recovered their losses, but were trading at record levels.

The causes of the Asian flu, as it was later billed, were large and complex, but boil down to investors choosing to ignore basic economic fundamentals. In Thailand the banks made two of the most cardinal mistakes in finance – to believe what politicians say, and to believe their own propaganda.

The Thai government had repeatedly insisted that the national currency, the baht, would remain fixed against the United States dollar, against the forces of economic logic. Because there were not enough baht in circulation to pay for the wild expansion of new property and resort developments, industrial projects, and other speculative ventures, the private banks borrowed dollars from international institutions known as hedge funds offering them derivatives which were based on the '*guaranteed*' (sic) future success of the businesses they were funding. Having talked up the potential profit of these ventures to dollar funders, the bankers believed in them. A further complication was that many of the new ventures were headed by friends of the bankers – leading to the charge of 'crony capitalism'.

Martin Feldstein, formerly chairman of the United States' President's Council of Economic Advisers and now professor of economics at Harvard University, later wrote a cogent analysis of the problem, which I believe is worth reading for it shows clearly the interdependence that has become the essential factor of globalisation. His précis is simple and logical.*

Thailand, the first country to succumb to the Asian financial 'flu' in 1997, offers a classic example of a current account crisis. Thailand fixed its exchange rate at 25 baht to the dollar in 1987 and promised to use whatever policies were necessary to keep it there. But by the mid-1990s the baht was grossly overvalued, causing a current account deficit – the trade deficit plus the net interest due on foreign debts – equal to 8 per cent of Thailand's gross domestic product, one of the highest anywhere in the world. A current account deficit must be financed with an equally large inflow of funds from the rest of the world. Because the Thai government promised a fixed baht–dollar exchange rate, Thai

---

A Self-Help Guide for Emerging Markets, by Martin Feldstein. Foreign Affairs, March/April 1999.

banks and businesses felt comfortable borrowing dollars to finance activities in Thailand. Similarly foreign creditors were willing to lend in order to reap the yields of the slightly higher Thai interest rates. The banks and the foreign lenders did recognise the risk they were taking: the huge current account deficit could be sustained only as long as foreign investors and lenders kept sending money to Thailand and increasing their total Thai exposure. If the day came when they were no longer willing to do so, the current-account would have to shrink to whatever could be financed with available capital inflows. In turn, reducing the current account deficit would require a fall in the baht to make Thai exports cheaper and imports more expensive. The cheaper baht would hurt those Thai banks and businesses that had borrowed in dollars. Foreigners who had lent baht would also lose, as would those who had lent dollars to Thai banks and businesses now unable to repay their dollar obligations.

In 1997 this potential risk became a reality. Eventually fear began to outweigh greed and foreigners became too nervous to keep lending. As the baht began to fall, other skittish investors with baht assets sold baht as well. Others borrowed baht on the assumption that the baht would continue to slide. The government tried to support the currency, but eventually exhausted its foreign reserves. By the time the baht stopped falling, it had plummeted by more than half.

The big lesson to be learned from these events is that as we enter the new millennium we live in a global economy, and that no one politician, however powerful or popular in his own country, can hope to influence the ebb and flow of world money. True power now lies with the markets, which dictate the fate of countries large and small. And in turn the markets are in the hands of the money masters and the money minders, men and women to whom, directly or indirectly, we have entrusted our savings. If they do not like the policies of a government, do not rate the performance of a corporation's executive, or do not believe that a country or company has the best interest of investors at heart, they can move the money in their care, at whim, within seconds, to anywhere they like. With globalization, capital may be shifted to whichever country offers the best investment opportunities.

Globalization of financial markets and the world of business has led many intellectuals to question its power. These critics inevitably include both the new Left and unreconstructed Marxists, but there are also others who support the capitalist system but nonetheless see dangers in untrammelled opportunism.

These critics frequently quote the collapse in Russia in the late nineties as an example of where globalization has failed. Certainly capitalism has been less than an unqualified success in the former Soviet Union. But that is not a testimony to the efficacy of the communist system, which foundered in shame and disrepute.

The introduction of capitalism and share ownership in Russia was woefully mismanaged. Judgements made at every level were poor. By issuing free shares to citizens and then permitting them to sell them at modest profits, Moscow's Western advisers ensured that the former communist apparachiks and the black market racketeers picked up control of many industries at low cost. International banks compounded the error by lending money to these same people on the strength of business plans that forecast strong future earnings – in other words, by issuing junk bonds.

In most cases these earnings failed to materialize, and the money was not paid back, some of it vanishing through money laundering in Switzerland and other tax havens. Those who had investments to support genuine proposals in inefficient industries found that there were few customers for their products. In particular the former Comecon countries turned against Russian goods, however cheap, preferring to buy from Germany, France, Britain and the United States.

And those who put hard currency into potentially successful businesses in Russia, such as hotels, restaurants and media, saw the value of their investments eroded, with the meagre profits being almost worthless in dollar terms.

The International Monetary Fund provided a partial bailout to the Russian government headed by the mercurial President Boris Yeltzin, but by the time the annual meeting of the Fund came round in 1999, the IMF members were wringing their hands as to what to do about Russia and the disappearance of billions of dollars' worth of funds. Sceptical members of the United States Congress, who had questioned the wisdom of the bailout, were livid.

Was this a failure of globalization? Probably not. It was more a question of banker greed. Financial institutions were seeking too large a return too quickly, rather than being prepared for a slower but more enduring payback, which would have necessitated this involvement at board level and in management to get things right.

When some leading world leaders pondered this question in Davos in the winter of 1999 they quickly agreed that globalization needed more transparency, improved accountability, stronger banking systems, better risk management, more information and better supervision. But who would make this happen? No one was sure. No one was really convinced the existing institutions were anywhere near providing the right framework. But no one was sure what might replace them. As I conclude this edition, this issue is still being hotly debated.

Index